THE SOUTHERN KURILE ISLANDS: SHROUDED IN ETERNAL FOG

There is a long standing territorial dispute between Japan and Russia over four islands in the Kurile archipelago. This dispute is the primary reason that the two countries have not, to this day, signed a peace treaty after World War II. The dispute has dominated the relations between the two countries for the last half century and for the most part can be characterized by two diametrically opposed, intractable positions. It continues to shape their foreign policy toward each other today.

The Kurile archipelago consists of 22 volcanic islands and numerous additional islets and rocks. It stretches for 1,300 kilometers from the northeast corner of the Japanese island of Hokkaido in a northeast direction to the southern tip of the Russian Kamchatka peninsula and separates the northern Pacific Ocean from the Sea of Okhotsk.

There are four disputed islands: Etorofu, Kunashiri, Shikotan, and Habomai shoto, collectively referred to in Russian as the Southern Kuriles and in Japanese as the Northern Territories. In this paper they are referred to as the disputed islands.[1] These islands are in the immediate proximity of Hokkaido and are relatively small, about the size of the second smallest U.S. state, Delaware.[2] The islands are challenged with harsh winters and are blanketed in fog throughout the summer months.

Until the days immediately following World War II,[3] they always were under Japanese jurisdiction and universally recognized as such, as established by the 1855 Treaty of Shimoda. The Russian Federation (and previously the Soviet Union) has administered the islands since their occupation in September 1945. At that time 17,291 Japanese were repatriated. Today, with the exception of the Habomai islets, the islands are occupied by almost 20,000 Russians, most working in the fishing and fish processing industries or part of the Russian military or Border Guard.

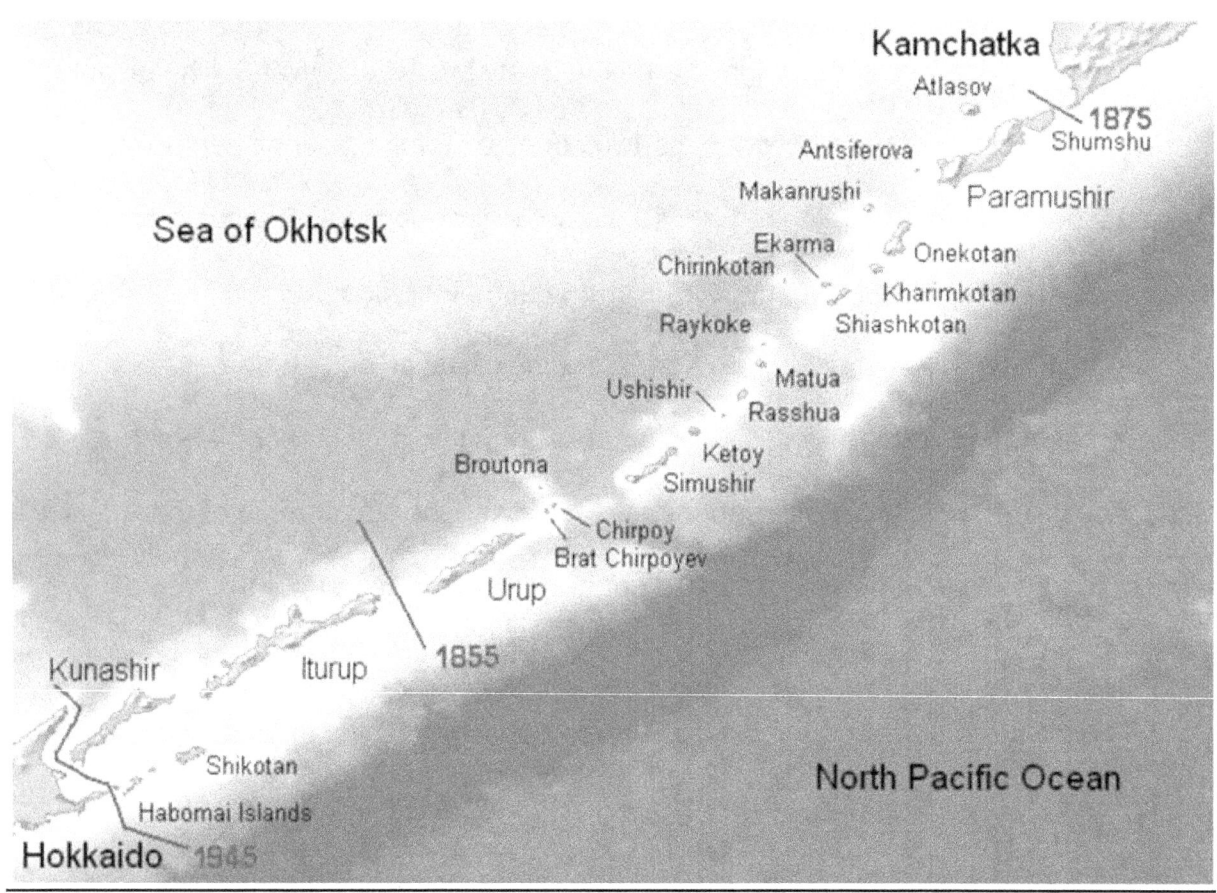

Figure 1. Kurile Archipelago with Lines of Demarcation and Administration by Date[4]

The Kurile archipelago was strategically important to the Soviet Union because it is the gateway between the northern Pacific Ocean, the Sea of Okhotsk and Russia's Far East. Today the disputed islands are important to both Russia and Japan because of the rich fishing grounds surrounding them.[5] The disputed islands are important to Japan from a domestic perspective. Japanese are very loyal, proud, and nationalistic people. They believe they have legal authority for sovereignty over the islands and are steadfast in this position. Opposed are the Russians, which are also a proud society. Most important to Russians, they have physical possession of the islands, which they gained during World War II as a result of an agreement amongst the Allies in 1945 at Yalta. The islands were a prize to the Soviet Union for entering the war in Asia against Japan.

The territorial dispute is a strategic interest to the United States for several reasons. The United States and Japan are strong allies; they have a bi-lateral security agreement and are significant trading partners. Second, the peace and stability of the Asia-Pacific region can benefit from positive relations between Japan and Russia. Finally, a resolution of this dispute could serve as a model for resolving other maritime island disputes in the Pacific, which would enhance stability in the region.[6]

The dispute has its origins in the Soviet occupation of the disputed islands in the days immediately following World War II. However, the background is much older. It is necessary to understand the early history of the region and the treaties that pre-date World War II. John J. Stephan's book, *The Kurile Islands: Russo-Japanese Frontiers in the Pacific,*[7] is a very comprehensive history.[8] The author relied heavily on Hiroshi Kimura's comprehensive work, *The Kurillian Knot: A History of Japanese-Russian Border Negotiations,*[9] since it illustrates the history of the dispute through the description of 42 historical documents that form the official record for negotiation of a settlement, as agreed upon by Russia and Japan in 1992 and 2001, referred to as the Joint Compendium.[10]

Historical Background

In the seventeenth century, Japanese began exploring Hokkaido and its neighboring islands, which were the home of the indigenous Ainu population. In 1821, the Russian Tsar issued an Imperial Decree which defined and claimed the Kurile Islands from Kamchatka to, and including, the island of Urup. [11] The four islands to the south were not claimed. In 1852, Tsar Nicholas I provided guidance his military representative that affirmed the 1821 extent of Russian territory and acknowledged the four islands as Japanese.[12] In 1855, Japan and Russia concluded the Treaty of Shimoda, which officially established the border by stating, "Henceforth the boundary between Russia and Japan will pass between the islands of Etorofu and Uruppu."[13]

The Treaty of Shimoda did not establish any sovereignty over the island of Sakhalin, to the northwest of Hokkaido and not part of the Kurile archipelago. Sakhalin was jointly administered for 20 years. However, conflicts and disputes led to the 1875 St. Petersburg Treaty, which exchanged the Kurile Islands for Sakhalin. The treaty specifically listed the Kurile Islands, which included all the islands from Kamchatka to Urup. It did not include the four southern islands currently in dispute.[14]

A treaty in 1895 superseded the 1855 Treaty of Shimoda without alteration. A subsequent Declaration of clarification upheld the validity of the 1875 Treaty of St. Petersburg. Thus, at the turn of the century, by treaty, Russia maintained sovereignty over the entire island of Sakhalin and Japan held sovereignty to all the islands between Hokkaido and Kamchatka.

Following the Russo-Japanese War of 1904-1905, the Portsmouth Peace Treaty ceded the southern portion of the island of Sakhalin to Japan by establishing a border at 50 degrees latitude.[15] There was no change to Japan's sovereignty over the Kurile Islands. Following clashes on Sakhalin in 1920 and Japan's subsequent occupation of the entire island, Japan and the USSR concluded an agreement that reaffirmed the

Treaty of Portsmouth and resulted in the withdrawal of Japanese forces from the northern half of Sakhalin.[16]

In 1941, Japan and the Soviet Union signed a neutrality pact.[17] The Atlantic Charter of August 14, 1941 was a joint declaration by President Theodore Roosevelt and Prime Minister Winston Churchill that established the principle of no territorial expansion. The Soviet Union acceded to the Charter on September 24, 1941.[18]

Two years later, on November 27, 1943, the United States, Great Britain, and the Republic of China signed the joint Cairo Declaration, which reaffirmed the principle of no territorial expansion.[19] Two points are critical with respect to the Cairo Declaration. It was simply a statement of purpose and intent by its signatories, which did not include the Soviet Union or Japan. Second, Japanese sovereignty of the disputed islands was peacefully and mutually established by the 1855 Treaty of Shimoda.[20]

On February 11, 1945, Roosevelt, Churchill, and Josef Stalin signed the secret Yalta Agreement,[21] which stated,

> "The leaders of the three Great Powers - the Soviet Union, the United States of America and Great Britain - have agreed that in two or three months after Germany has surrendered and the war in Europe has terminated the Soviet Union shall enter into the war against Japan on the side of the Allies on condition that:...2. The former rights of Russia violated by the treacherous attack of Japan in 1904 shall be restored, viz: (a) the southern part of Sakhalin as well as all the islands adjacent to it shall be returned to the Soviet Union,...3. The Kurile Islands shall be handed over to the Soviet Union...The Heads of the three Great Powers have agreed that these claims of the Soviet Union shall be unquestionably fulfilled after Japan has been defeated."[22]

The significance of the Yalta Agreement cannot be overstated. However, it was a statement between three leaders in 1945; it has no legal binding on Japan.[23] For clarification, the Preface to the first edition of the Joint Compendium states,

"The Soviet Union maintained that the Yalta Agreement provided legal confirmation of the transfer of the Kurile Islands to the USSR, including the islands of Etorofu, Kunashiri, Shikotan and Habomai. Japan's position is that the Yalta Agreement is not the final determination on the territorial issue and that Japan, which is not party to this Agreement, is neither legally nor politically bound by its provisions."[24]

The Soviet Union formally denounced the neutrality pact with Japan on April 5, 1945.[25] On July 26, 1945, the United States, China, and Great Britain issued the Potsdam Declaration, providing Japan with terms for its unconditional surrender.[26] However, the Potsdam Declaration did not provide a clear and indisputable definition of what territory Japan would maintain if it accepted the declaration's conditions.

On August 6, 1945, the United States struck Hiroshima with the first atomic bomb. On August 8, 1945, the Soviet Union issued an announcement that accepted the proposition of the Potsdam Declaration and formally declared war with Japan, effective the following day.[27] On August 9, 1945, the United States dropped the second atomic bomb on Nagasaki.

On August 15, a recorded message of the Emperor of Japan, the Imperial Rescript on the Termination of the War, was broadcast to the Japanese people. It announced the acceptance of the Potsdam Declaration, through which the Cairo Declaration became legally binding upon Japan.

The events of World War II produced three instances with ambiguous definitions of the "Kurile Islands." They were the negotiations between the USSR and Japan surrounding a nonaggression or neutrality pact, the Yalta Agreement, and the Potsdam Declaration. These documents failed to provide a clear definition of the exact scope of the "Kurile Islands." As a result, confusion, various interpretations, and a lack of consensus exist to this day. Furthermore, the United States added to this confusion in two more instances following World War II.

On August 17, the United States issued General Order Number 1 to General MacArthur, providing him with guidance for the Japanese surrender. In particular, it listed which areas would surrender to which allied forces. With respect to Japan and the Kurile Islands, it stated, "The Imperial General Headquarters…in the main islands of Japan, minor islands adjacent thereto…shall surrender to the Commander in Chief, U.S. Army Forces in the Pacific." The United States staffed the order with the allies. Stalin approved but made two additional requests for clarification: to include all of the Kurile Islands in the area of the surrender of Japanese armed forces to Soviet troops in accordance with the Yalta Conference, and that the northern part of Hokkaido would be occupied by the Soviets. On August 18, Roosevelt responded by agreeing that all the Kurile Islands would become Soviet territory, but refused the request for the Soviet occupation of Hokkaido.[28]

Kimura provides a substantial argument that the definition of "all of the Kurile Islands" was not explicitly known or agreed upon. He provides two sources, both Japanese, which suggest that Soviet field commanders were under the impression that their occupation of the Kurile Islands was to proceed as far south as Urup, and not further to Etorofu, Kunashiri, Shikotan, and the Habomai islets.[29] In the absence of a U.S. troop presence, the Soviets occupied the disputed islands between August 28 and September 5.[30]

The second instance occurred in the beginning of 1946. General MacArthur's Directive Number 677 of January 29, 1946, *Memorandum from the Commander-in-*

Chief of the Allied Forces to the Japanese Imperial Government, defined Japan as its four main islands and approximately 1,000 smaller adjacent islands, excluding many others that it stated explicitly. The Kurile Islands, the Habomai Island Group and Shikotan Island were included among the exceptions.[31] There is a very important distinction in this statement, which continues to this day to contribute significantly to varying perspectives of the disputed islands. The wording infers that the Habomai Island Group and Shikotan are not part of the definition of the Kurile Islands.[32]

On February 2, 1946, the Soviet Union responded, by issuing the *Decree of the Presidium of the USSR Supreme Soviet on the Creation of the South-Sakhalin Province in the Khabarovsk Region*, which stated, "Create on the territory of South Sakhalin and the Kurile Islands the South Sakhalin province."[33] In 1947, the South-Sakhalin Province was abolished by incorporating it in the Sakhalin Province, and on February 25, 1947, an amendment to the Soviet constitution made the Sakhalin Province part of the Russian Republic.[34]

Thus, in the years following World War II, the Soviet Union had possession of southern Sakhalin, previously lost to Japan in the Russo-Japanese War of 1905 in accordance with the Portsmouth Peace Treaty, the northern Kuriles, which were previously ceded to Japan in the St. Petersburg Treaty of 1875, and the four disputed islands, which were established as Japanese in the 1855 Treaty of Shimoda.[35] It is important to note that the Soviet occupation gave them possession and administration of these areas, but the Soviet Union did not have legal authority, which can only be transferred through a treaty, in accordance with the principles of international law.[36]

Early in 1951 the United States, Great Britain, the Soviet Union, Japan, and numerous other countries prepared for the San Francisco Peace Conference to resolve the Pacific theater of World War II. In March, the United States and Britain prepared a draft agreement that upheld the intent of the Yalta Agreement that the Soviet Union would gain sovereignty over southern Sakhalin and the Kurile Islands as a reward for entering the war against Japan. However, for other reasons, the draft was not satisfactory to the Soviet Union.[37]

The San Francisco Peace Conference met in September 1951, and the Allies and Japan signed the multi-lateral Treaty of Peace with Japan.[38] The Soviet Union sent a delegation, but did not sign the treaty. This left the status of the islands in question. The treaty stipulated that Japan forfeit its sovereign claims, but did not say to whom. This position is underscored by statements made at the Conference by the delegates of three principle nations, the United States as the primary architect of the treaty, the Soviet Union, and Japan.[39]

The statement of the U.S. delegate, John Foster Dulles, upheld the primacy of the Potsdam Declaration, implied that the Yalta Agreement does not apply to Japan, and stated the U.S. position that the Habomai Islands are part of the "minor islands" of Hokkaido, over which Japan retains sovereignty.[40] The speech by the Soviet delegate, Andrey Gromyko, provides evidence that he understood that the San Francisco Peace Treaty should have resolved the sovereignty of the islands, but that it did not, and supports the idea that Japan cannot renounce its own sovereignty over a particular territory without also recognizing someone else's sovereignty over that same territory.[41]

Prime Minister Shigeru Yoshida's statement reinforced the idea that southern Sakhalin and the Kurile Islands were obtained legally and peacefully and that Japan was always recognized as having sovereignty over Etorofu and Kunashiri. It also implied that Habomai islets and Shikotan were always Japanese as an extension of Hokkaido.[42] His interpretations are in agreement with both Dulles' statement and the earlier MacArthur Declaration Number 677.

Kimura describes the Soviet decision to not sign the San Francisco Peace Treaty as a mistake and quotes four Soviet and Russian sources, including Nikita Khrushchev, who provided the same critique as early as 1965.[43]

Japan made its first mistake when a senior bureaucrat of the Ministry of Foreign Affairs responded to the question, "What exactly is meant by the Kurile Islands?"[44] during a meeting of the Japanese Diet on October 19, 1951. His initial answer was that the Northern and the Southern Kuriles were included in the definition in the peace treaty.[45] This dialogue confirmed the confusion over the definition of the Kurile Islands in the San Francisco Peace Treaty[46] and reinforced the Soviet interpretation, which was upheld until Mikhail Gorbachev came to power.

In 1956, U.S. Secretary of State Dulles provided an expanded U.S. position on the disputed islands, specifically that "Etorofu and Kunashiri (along with the Habomai Islands and Shikotan, which are part of Hokkaido) have always been a part of Japan proper and should in justice be acknowledged as under Japanese sovereignty."[47]

After Stalin's death in 1953, the Soviet Union embarked on a new foreign policy of peaceful co-existence, and Khrushchev had consolidated his power by 1956. Ichirō Hatoyama became the Prime Minister of Japan in 1954 and sought a more independent stance from the United States. In particular he wanted to establish relations with the Soviet Union. Thus, the two new leaders created a ripe climate for new opportunities for Soviet – Japanese relations.

Talks on the normalization of relations between the Soviet Union and Japan began in 1955 and continued into 1956. At three different sets of meetings, the Soviets offered a two island solution, the return of Habomai and Shikotan, to which Japan countered with requests for the return of all four islands.[48]

In an effort to establish relations with the Soviet Union, Hatoyama traveled to Moscow in October 1956. The two sides issued the Soviet-Japanese Joint Declaration, which normalized diplomatic relations. It was not a peace treaty and it did not resolve the territorial dispute. Most importantly, it specifically described the Soviet position of returning Habomai and Shikotan, but it did not detail the Japanese position which considered all four islands to be in dispute. In fact, it stated that negotiations toward a peace treaty would continue, but it didn't specify negotiations of the territorial dispute.[49] Article 9 of the Joint Declaration stated,

> "9. Japan and the Union of Soviet Socialist Republics agree to continue, after the restoration of normal diplomatic relations between Japan and the Union of Soviet Socialist Republics, negotiations for the conclusion of a peace treaty. The Union of Soviet Socialist Republics, desiring to meet the wishes of Japan and taking into consideration the interests of Japan, agrees to hand over to Japan the Habomai Islands and the island of Shikotan. However, the actual handing over these islands to Japan shall take place after the conclusion of a peace treaty between Japan and the Union of Soviet Socialist Republics."[50]

The Soviet position for the remainder of the Cold War upheld the 1956 Joint Declaration. In particular, the Soviets adopted the position that the territorial dispute no longer existed.[51] In other words, the 1956 Declaration had resolved the dispute by agreeing that the Soviet Union would transfer Habomai and Shikotan at the conclusion of a peace treaty. In effect, the Soviets adopted the position that there was nothing remaining to negotiate.[52] The fact that Japan allowed a joint declaration that stated the Soviet two island offer and did not state the Japanese four island position was Japan's second significant mistake in the short span of only five years.

In 1960, after the United States and Japan revised their Treaty of Cooperation and Security, the Soviet Union protested by sending Japan a memorandum that unilaterally placed additional conditions on the 1956 Joint Declaration.[53] The memorandum protested the continued U.S. troop presence in Japan and declared,

> "the Soviet Government finds it necessary to declare that the islands of Habomai and Shikotan will be handed over to Japan, as was stated in the Soviet-Japanese Joint Declaration of October 19, 1956, only if all foreign troops are withdrawn from Japan and a Soviet-Japanese peace treaty is signed."[54]

Japan issued a memorandum in response that made three points. First, it upheld the 1956 Joint Declaration, "It is an official international document which has been ratified by the highest organs of both countries. It is needless to say that the contents of this solemn international undertaking cannot be changed unilaterally."[55] Second, it stated that U.S. troops were stationed in Japan in 1956, at the time of the signing of the Joint Declaration, and this absolved Japan of the charges of changing anything or of provoking the Soviet Union. Third, Japan emphasized its position with respect to all the disputed islands, "Our country will keep insisting on the reversion not only of the islands of Habomai and Shikotan but also of the other islands which are inherent parts of Japanese territory."[56]

Gorbachev: Some Improvements on the Periphery

The six year period of Mikhail Gorbachev's administration, from 1985 to 1991, can be described as one of dramatic changes in Soviet domestic and international affairs.[57] In both Japan and the USSR, attitudes and perceptions toward each other improved.[58] Public opinion polls show that the number of Japanese who were favorable to the Soviet Union rose from 8.6% in June 1985 to 25.4% in October 1991.[59] In addition, economic cooperation increased during this period. However, with respect to the disputed islands, there were some positive improvements on the periphery but no significant developments toward resolution. The period was characterized by continuity in policy toward the territorial dispute as much as by change in all other areas.[60] By the time President Gorbachev finally visited Japan in April 1991 for the first USSR – Japan summit, the opportunity for significant progress in the territorial dispute had slipped away.[61]

There were several positive developments[62] resulting from an increase in Ministerial visits from about one per decade to a visit almost yearly.[63] In May 1986, both sides agreed that Japanese could visit graves in the disputed islands without the use of passports. Later that year the first visits in over a decade were made. There were reciprocal visits by Soviets in December 1986.[64] In December 1988, both sides agreed to establish a permanent working group towards a peace treaty. During a visit to Moscow by the Japanese Foreign Minister in May 1989, the Soviets said that, "it is possible to conclude a peace treaty even under the Japan-United States Security Treaty."[65] This rolled back the unilateral Soviet declaration of 1960.

Cultural exchanges and economic ties were increasing as well. Japan was the Soviet Union's largest Asian trading partner; five times larger than the Soviet Union's next largest Asian trading partner, South Korea. Japan even ranked in the top five of all of the Soviet Union's trading partners. In May 1986, the two countries signed an

Agreement on Cultural Exchanges to further expand exchanges in a reciprocal and balanced manner.[66] In the May 1989, Japan proposed a policy of "balanced expansion or expanded equilibrium" instead of the principle of "inseparability of economics and politics."[67]

In April 1991, President Gorbachev visited Japan. The result was a joint communiqué that officially reversed the long held Soviet position that the 1956 Joint Declaration resolved the territorial dispute, a position consistently espoused by Andrei Gromyko, the Soviet Foreign Minister from 1957 to 1985. Furthermore, it recognized that the dispute includes all four islands, not just Habomai and Shikotan. The Communiqué described the summit as,

> "...in-depth and thorough negotiations on a whole range of issues relating to the preparation and conclusion of a peace treaty between Japan and the Union of Soviet Socialist Republics, including the issue of territorial demarcation, taking into consideration the positions of both sides on the attribution of the islands of Habomai, Shikotan, Kunashiri, and Etorofu."[68]

The Communiqué also specifically agreed to several additional measures, including a reduction of Soviet military forces,[69]

> "...expand exchanges between residents of Japan and residents of the aforementioned islands, to establish a simplified visa-free framework for visits by the Japanese to these islands, to initiate joint, mutually beneficial economic activities in that region, and to reduce the Soviet military forces stationed on these islands...Cooperation should take place in trade-economic, scientific-technological, and political spheres as well as in social, cultural, educational, tourism, and sports realms through free and wide-ranging exchanges between the citizens of the two countries."[70]

Unfortunately the summit did not produce any dramatic results for a resolution of the disputed islands. Kimura asserts that Gorbachev's visit was poorly timed. Had he visited earlier and taken more initiative toward establishing a peace treaty, he may have been able to gain significant economic assistance from Japan.[71]

14

Yeltsin Years: Improvements Followed by the Lost Opportunity

During Boris Yeltsin's first visit to Japan in January 1990 as a deputy of the Supreme Soviet,[72] he proposed a five stage solution to the territorial dispute. The steps were: 1) the Soviet Union acknowledge the territorial dispute, 2) designate the islands as a joint, free enterprise zone, 3) demilitarize the islands, 4) sign a peace treaty, and 5) a final solution of either joint administration, independent free status, or reversion to Japanese sovereignty, to be determined at the "discretion of a new generation."[73] This preceded Mikhail Gorbachev's summit in April 1991, and therefore was the first public acknowledgement of a territorial dispute since 1956, albeit unofficially. However, the five step proposal sequenced a peace treaty prior to the final determination of the islands' sovereignty. This was problematic since a peace treaty is the instrument to legally establish sovereignty.

In May 1990, Yeltsin was elected by committee vote as Chairman of the Presidium of the Supreme Soviet of the Russian Soviet Federative Socialist Republic. He was a vocal critic and opponent of Gorbachev and exerted his influence when possible. Prior to Gorbachev's April 1991 summit, Yeltsin urged Gorbachev not to concede on the territorial dispute.[74] It appears that Yeltsin was seeking economic cooperation as a pre-condition to resolving the dispute, most likely because the Russian domestic economy was undergoing a serious downturn as a result of the political and economic reforms. For example, in 1990 the GDP fell by 2% and in 1991 it would fall by 17%, the first negative rates since WWII.[75]

In June 1991, by popular vote Yeltsin became the first democratically elected President of the Russian Soviet Federative Socialist Republic. He sent a private letter to the Japanese Prime Minister in September 1991 that reversed the long held Soviet position that the islands in dispute were Soviet possessions resulting from war. He offered that "judging international politics in terms of victors and vanquished is an anachronism" and "the territorial dispute should be settled on the basis of law and justice." He reiterated the five stage proposal and said that the "conclusion of a peace treaty is a matter of urgency."[76]

The following month, the Japanese Foreign Minister visited Moscow and "informed the Russian government that if it recognized Japanese sovereignty over the islands, Tokyo was prepared to be flexible about the timing, manner, and conditions of their reversion."[77]

In November 1991, in a letter to the Russian people, Yeltsin summarized his concept of Russia's interaction in the global world by stating, "an obvious obligation of the new Russian leadership is to look for ways of resolving problems which we inherited from the policies of previous eras,...and thus make legality, justice and strict adherence to the principles of international law the criteria of its policy."[78] With specific regard to Russo-Japanese relations, he stated,

> "it would be unforgivable to continue to endure a situation where relations with Japan remain practically frozen because of the absence of a peace treaty between the two countries... the main obstacle to the conclusion of this treaty is the issue of the demarcation of borders...we will be guided by the principles of justice and humanism, and we will firmly defend the interests and dignity of Russians including those of the inhabitants of the Southern Kuriles...no inhabitant of the Southern Kuriles will see their future ruined. Their socio-economic and property interests will be fully provided for..."[79]

Thus, Yeltsin supported an approach for a solution rooted in legality, justice, international law, and "humanism," which he further defined as protecting the individual interests of the Russian inhabitants of the disputed islands.

In December 1991 the Soviet Union dissolved, the Commonwealth of Independent States was formed, and the Russian Republic became the Russian Federation.

Peace Treaty Working Group and ministerial meetings were held in February and March 1992. The Japanese government stated it would not require the repatriation of Russian citizens immediately upon recognition of Japanese sovereignty and that the Russian inhabitants could be given the opportunity to remain and become Japanese citizens.[80] Additionally, the meetings resulted in agreements to begin mutual visits between the disputed islands and the Japanese mainland and to issue a joint compendium on the history of the territorial issue between Japan and Russia.[81]

Exchanges without visas began in April 1992 between the northern islands and the Japanese mainland. Between 1992 and 2008, 8,853 Japanese have visited the islands and 6,691 Russians have visited Japan.[82] The Japanese Ministry of Foreign Affairs description of the 1992 visits follows,

> "As a result, frank dialogue between the Russian residents in the northern territories and the Japanese citizens was realized for the first time in history. This has produced a positive outcome in alleviating concern of the Russian residents in the four islands and promoting their understanding of Japan's standpoint."[83]

In the summer of 1992, meetings were held to prepare for a September 1992 summit. At a meeting between Yeltsin and the Japanese Foreign Minister, Yeltsin "for the first time promised complete withdrawal of Russian military forces stationed in the four northern islands in the near future."[84] Demilitarization was the third step in Yeltsin's five stage proposal.

At the same time, there were rising domestic concerns over the reversion of the islands to Japan. At a public hearing held by Supreme Soviet in July 1992, the Russian

Foreign Ministry attempted to defend the principle of law and justice and the recent positive developments between Russia and Japan. However, four days prior to the September summit, Yeltsin postponed his visit to Japan, citing domestic concerns as the reason.[85] Kimura describes "three primary factors behind the cancellation, namely, the resurgence of conservative forces in Russia, the eruption of nationalism, and the weakening of Yeltsin's leadership."[86] Jeffrey Mankoff attributes the cancellation to pressure exerted by "hard-liners in the Supreme Soviet and the military."[87] The effect on the Japanese is best described by the results of a poll in October – November 1992. There was a decrease in the number of Japanese respondents that were favorably disposed to the Soviet Union to 15.2%; the percentage was 25.4% the year prior.[88]

Originally planned to be released at the summit, the two Foreign Ministers announced the publication of the first edition of the *Joint Compendium of Documents on the History of Territorial Issue between Japan and Russia* while at the 47th Session of the UN General Assembly later in September.[89] The Joint Compendium consists of a preface and 35 documents from 1644 to 1991.[90]

A year later, in October 1993, Yeltsin did visit Japan for a summit, resulting in the Tokyo Declaration. It reiterated the recognition of the territorial dispute involving "Etorofu, Kunashiri, Shikotan and Habomai," committed both parties to a solution "on the basis of historical and legal facts" and "the principles of law and justice," recognized the Joint Compendium, pledged continued mutual visits, emphasized economic cooperation and free trade, and agreed to continued meetings with the purpose of fully normalizing their bi-lateral relationship.

This was a significant declaration since it codified in one document many of the incremental steps that had taken place in the last decade. Furthermore, it established the basis for future negotiations. Specifically, Article 2 of the Tokyo Declaration states,

> "Both sides agree that negotiations toward an early conclusion of a peace treaty through the solution of this issue on the basis of historical and legal facts and based on the documents produced with the two countries' agreement as well as on the principles of law and justice should continue."[91]

Kimura emphasizes the importance of the "basis of historical and legal facts" and "principles of law and justice." He further notes that "documents produced with the two countries' agreement" specifically refer to the *Joint Compendium*.[92]

However, in other statements, Yeltsin imposed what Kimura describes as a "double barrier" of "closing the gap" and "preparing the environment." Kimura assessed Yeltsin as "implying that Japan was not doing enough to improve relations between the two countries, and that even if it were, the Russian people were still far from mentally prepared to hand over the islands."[93]

Unfortunately the best opportunity to resolve the conflict was lost to Yeltsin's concept of an incremental phased approach, as articulated in the five stage proposal, rather than a single comprehensive solution that would fully normalize relations between the countries via a peace treaty. This would have resolved the territorial dispute and opened the door for significant economic cooperation. Yeltsin most likely thought that the Russian population needed to be convinced first, through a strategy of significant economic assistance. In addition, economic ties with Japan were an important part of "Russia's foreign policy, as its priority shifted from conventional political and military aspects to the economic one."[94]

19

Japan was taking some economic steps, probably deemed sufficient, especially in light of the economic recession that began in 1990 and is described as Japan's "lost decade." Furthermore, Japan demonstrated flexibility in the "timing, manner, and conditions" of a reversion and had acknowledged Yeltsin's call for "humanism." From their perspective, the next step was for Russia to recognize Japanese sovereignty over the islands. Thus, both sides came very close but were unable to get to the final step of a resolution.

Two events worthy of mentioning occurred in 1994. In August a Russian Coast Guard vessel fired upon two Japanese fishing boats in "Russian" waters in the vicinity of the disputed islands.[95] One boat was damaged and one Japanese crew member wounded. It was reported that warning shots were fired and ignored.[96] Incidents of this nature can unnecessarily escalate and are damaging to the possibility of successful negotiations in the future.

In October a large earthquake of magnitude 8.1 occurred just east of Hokkaido and south east of the disputed islands. There was a local tsunami that caused additional damage. Eleven fatalities were reported in the contested islands and Hokkaido. Twice Japan provided humanitarian relief goods to the disputed islands.[97] In this instance, the response was beneficial to developing a positive, cooperative climate between both sides.

In 1996, the policies of the two countries toward each other continued to be misaligned. It is best described by the Japanese Ministry of Foreign Affairs assessment of the November 1996 Foreign Ministries meeting,

> "With regard to the issue of territorial sovereignty, Japan emphasized its
> view that Japan and Russia must press ahead simultaneously with both

territorial negotiations and efforts to create an environment conducive to the resolution of territorial issues. Russia put forward the idea (the details of which have not yet been fully studied) that both countries could engage in joint economic activities on the four islands while maintaining their respective positions regarding the sovereignty of these islands."[98]

Also in 1996, there was another incident involving the seizure of a Japanese fishing vessel.

1997 saw a change in Japanese policy toward Russia. Prime Minister Ryutaro Hashimoto announced in January an expanded, "multi-layered" approach that would "promote dialogue and cooperation with the country in various fields."[99] This rejuvenated the efforts toward a resolution and led to several agreements in the years following. In July of that year, "Prime Minister Hashimoto put forward the three principles of trust, mutual benefit and a long-term perspective with regard to Japan's foreign policy toward Russia," which was "greeted favorably by the Russian Government, mass media and so on."[100] In addition, the first Defense Ministry visit between the two countries took place.

These improvements opened the door for three successive summits in 1997 and 1998. The first two were informal and therefore nicknamed the "no neck tie" summits. In November 1997, Prime Minister Hashimoto met President Yeltsin in Krasnoyarsk, Siberia. Yeltsin proposed a goal of resolving the conflict by 2000 and concluded an economic assistance and cooperation agreement called the "Hashimoto-Yeltsin Plan."[101] Japan announced its support of Russia joining the Asia-Pacific Economic Cooperation (APEC) organization.[102]

The leaders also agreed to consider joint military exercises in support of humanitarian operations.[103] The following year, the Russian Navy and the Japanese Self Defense Forces conducted joint search and rescue exercises.[104] Another result of the first informal summit was the February 1998 fishing agreement, which specifically delineated the agreed area surrounding the contested islands, within which Japanese vessels may fish.[105]

President Yeltsin met Prime Minister Hashimoto in Japan on April 18-19, 1998. Hashimoto made an unofficial proposal that has not been made public. Kimura's research concluded that Hashimoto proposed the determination of a border that recognized Japanese sovereignty over all four of the disputed islands, that Russia would "exercise transitional administrative rights," and that the timing of the reversion would be decided by the next generation.[106] "In the economic sector," both leaders "agreed to continue to steadily implement and expand the Hashimoto-Yeltsin Plan."[107]

The third summit was an official meeting between the new Japanese Prime Minister Keizō Obuchi and President Yeltsin in Moscow on November 12, 1998. Yeltsin answered Hashimoto's unofficial proposal of the previous summit. He remained steadfast to his position that a peace treaty should be concluded first, normalizing relations, and that the border be demarcated in a subsequent treaty.[108] The summit concluded with the Moscow Declaration,[109] which reaffirmed the agreements of the previous summits, reiterated the goal to resolve the conflict by 2000, committed both parties to cooperation in all areas of relations between the two countries, and emphasized the importance of the Hashimoto – Yeltsin Plan.[110] The declaration acknowledged the importance of resolving the conflict not only for their own relations, but also "to contribute to the peace and stability of the Asia Pacific region."[111] Two sub-committees were established for border demarcation and to explore possibilities of joint economic activities in the contested islands. Finally, as a result of the summit Japan announced additional economic measures including loans and emergency medical cooperation.

There was progress in many small areas during the later years of Yeltsin's Presidency. Access to the exclusive economic zone of the disputed islands for the purposes of fishing was established. A framework for visa free visits was established for former Japanese residents and their families. Defense cooperation was initiated and Russia offered a complete withdrawal of military forces from the disputed islands. Japan provided humanitarian assistance after the 1994 earthquake. And, economic cooperation was steadily increasing.

In addition, there were significant steps for the resolution of the territorial dispute. Russia adopted a policy based on law and justice. The first edition of the *Joint Compendium* was published. Japan recognized the need to respect the needs of the Russians living on the disputed islands and proposed a concept of Russian transitional administration after recognition of Japanese sovereignty. However and unfortunately, in the end, the efforts of 1997-1998 were a repeat performance of the disappointing 1992-1993 meetings and summit. Both countries held onto their concept of the implementation of the final steps necessary to resolve the territorial dispute and normalize relations in support of comprehensive economic cooperation.

Putin Years

In 2001, a new edition of the Joint Compendium was jointly agreed upon, adding another preface and seven documents from 1993 to 2000.[112] During the January 2003 Summit, the two countries agreed to the Japan-Russia Action Plan, establishing cooperation in several areas.[113]

On September 2, 2004, Prime Minister Jun'ichirō Koizumi viewed a few of the Habomai islets while onboard a Japanese Coast Guard vessel. He said, "I would like to utilize my experience here today when I meet with President Vladimir Putin of the Russian Federation. Without the resolution of the disputed islands issue, there will be no conclusion of a peace treaty between Japan and Russia."[114]

On July 7, 2005, Prime Minister Koizumi held a summit meeting with President Putin of the Russian Federation during his visit to Gleneagles, UK, while attending the G8 Gleneagles Summit. The two leaders agreed that President Putin would pay a visit to Japan from November 20 to 22. They welcomed the steady progress being made in a broad range of areas in Japan-Russia relations based on the "Japan-Russia Action Plan." They affirmed mutual strategic importance in constructing an oil pipeline to Russia's Pacific coast. They confirmed that although the disputed islands are a difficult issue, efforts would be made continuously towards a resolution of the issue under their political leadership, in particular through the effort of the foreign ministers and foreign ministry officials of each country.[115]

The Government of Japan decided to extend technical grant aid equivalent to 150 million yen to the Administration of the Sakhalin Region, Russian Federation, with a view to promoting its economic and social reforms. Notes Verbales to this effect were exchanged on February 22, 2006, affirming the importance Japan places on the cooperative relationship with the neighboring Sakhalin Region. Japan expected that the assistance would promote the understanding of Japan in the Sakhalin Region.[116] Assistance was repeated again in 2007.[117]

On August 16, 2006, a Russian Border Patrol vessel fired upon and seized a Japanese fishing vessel. One crewmember was killed and three crew members and the boat were seized.[118]

Medvedev and Recent Events

On November 1, 2010, Russian President Dmitry Medvedev visited Kunashiri Island.[119] It was the first ever visit by a Russian leader to the disputed islands. The visit was probably carefully timed. It preceded a summit of the Asia – Pacific Economic Cooperation (APEC) forum in Yokohama, Japan, by two weeks. The visit was most likely intended to signal three distinct groups. First, Medvedev provided reassurances of economic development to the Russian residents. Second, he most likely wanted to communicate Russia's renewed strength, due to increased oil revenues, to Japan. Finally, he probably wanted to communicate that same message of renewed Russian strength to the attendees of the APEC forum.

In December 2010, President Medvedev claimed the disputed islands as Russian territory and proposed a joint economic free trade zone during a live television interview. Japan promptly refused the proposal. In January and early February, Russia conducted three visits to the disputed islands by the First Deputy Prime Minister, the Deputy Defense Minister, and the Defense Minister. President Medvedev stated the visits were to promote development.[120]

Annually, on February 7, the day that the Treaty of Shimoda was signed in 1855, Japan celebrates the "Northern Territories Day," an official national holiday since 1981. In 2011, Japan responded in kind to the Russian visits by using the holiday to publicize its interest in the disputed islands via 75 full page newspaper advertisements.[121] Just like Medvedev's visit to Kunashiri, the timing was well choreographed. It preceded a visit to Russia by Japan's Foreign Minister by three days. The meeting between the two Foreign Ministers did not produce any tangible results and served to only publicly acknowledge that the dispute had become more entrenched and positions had hardened on both sides following Medvedev's visit in November 2010 and Japan's publicity campaign in February 2011.[122]

Military Interests: A Former Reality Replaced by Rhetoric and Demonstration

Prior to World War II, during the period that Japan maintained sovereignty over the entire archipelago, the Kurile islands were not part of the conflicts between Japan and first Russia and then later, the Soviet Union.[123] Stalin stated the value of the Kurile Island archipelago as the gateway between Siberia and the Pacific Ocean.[124] However, it is more likely that Stalin's interest was not strategic, but to avenge the losses of the Russo-Japanese war of 1904-1905.[125] This is supported by a statement of a Russian resident of Shikotan that the Kurile archipelago was not occupied with forces from 1963 to 1977.[126]

In 1977 and 1978, the Soviet Union militarized the islands of Kunashiri, Etorofu, and Shikotan with fuel and ammunition storage, specifically naval mines, sonar and radar facilities, airfields, and associated soldiers and sailors. The Soviets established two bases in the Kurile archipelago, one of which was in the Southern Kuriles, at Hipokappu Bay on the island of Etorofu.[127] The militarization occurred in coordination with the deployment of Soviet ballistic missile submarines (SSBNs) to Petropavlovsk, on the Kamchatka peninsula.[128] The militarization was designed to establish the Sea of Okhotsk as a safe haven for the SSBNs from U.S. attack submarines.[129]

Geoffrey Jukes convincingly argues that technological advances in the range of submarine launched ballistic missiles (SLBMs) and the advent of multiple warheads per

SLBM in the1980s had a decisive impact on the strategic importance of the Kuriles. Longer range SLBMs enabled the Soviet Northern Fleet in the Barents Sea to reach the western United States. In 1993, Russia and the United States concluded the Strategic Arms Reduction Treaty II (START II) agreement, and then the Strategic Offensive Reductions Treaty (SORT) in 2002, which limited the sizes of the nuclear triads and the number of nuclear warheads.[130] These reductions eliminate the likelihood of any future growth in the SSBN fleet size.[131] Thus, the military importance of the Southern Kurile islands as an impenetrable boundary to the Sea of Okhotsk safe haven is significantly decreased.[132] In 1990, as part of his five stage proposal, Yeltsin proposed demilitarizing the disputed islands, which was later included in Gorbachev's 1991 Communiqué. In the 1990s, Russia unilaterally reduced the forces in the disputed islands, probably due to budgetary constraints or as part of reform within the armed forces.[133]

Jukes provides further assessment of the military importance of the maritime straits between the Kurile Islands. First, he disputes the perception that the straits in the northern Kurile archipelago are frozen in the winter while the southern straits are not. Using Soviet maritime navigation atlases of water temperature and salinity and personal observation, he concludes that the southern straits are actually ice bound and the northern straits are not.[134] Second, and more significant, is the penetration of the Kurile archipelago by U.S. attack submarines, beginning in 1982.[135] The U.S. submarines transited four straits, moving between the Pacific Ocean and the Sea of Okhotsk to track the Soviet SSBNs. The most southern of those four straits is Friza Proliv (Vries Strait), between the islands of Urup and Etorofu; which is 35 kilometers wide and 625 meters (2050 feet) deep.[136]

Furthermore, Jukes makes the following two points. Concerns over the loss of control over particular straits can be mitigated by agreement between Russia and Japan. He mentions the 1936 Montreux Convention, which governs the Turkish Straits (Bosporus and Dardanelles) between the Black and Mediterranean seas.[137] Alternatively, the UN Convention on the Law of the Sea (UNCLOS) could also apply. Finally, a bi-lateral agreement between Japan and Russia could govern the future of military installations located on any land ceded from Russia to Japan. The agreement could provide for temporary or long term continuation of the use of airfields, radar sites, or sonar capabilities and stations. The terms of the agreement could provide financial assistance for the relocation of those facilities.[138] Jukes offers the German – Soviet agreement on bases in East Germany after German unification as an example.[139] The author adds the agreement between Japan and the United States for the relocation of Marines from Okinawa to Japan, which included Japanese financial assistance, as another example. An agreement of this sort would be critical to any change in the status of Etorofu, which includes an airfield, naval facility, radar and sonar facilities, and logistics stores.

Russian military concerns include the possibility of future use of the disputed islands by Japan or even the United States.[140] The long term basing of U.S. military forces in Japan contributed to the Soviet protest in 1960 against the U.S. - Japanese Treaty of Cooperation and Security. A treaty resolving the disputed islands could include guarantees of permanent demilitarization or agreements for reciprocal reductions in local military force levels.[141]

In early February 2011, President Medvedev announced a modernization initiative for Russia's military presence in the disputed islands. During a meeting with defense and regional development ministers, he stated, "Everybody must understand that the South Kurile Islands are Russian territory."[142] It is important to note the events surrounding this announcement. The period of November 2010 through February 2011 included President Medvedev's visit to the disputed islands, as well as three other visits and an increase in rhetoric on both sides. Furthermore, the announcement preceded by a few days a visit by the Japanese Foreign Minister to Moscow. Military modernization is meant to signal Russia's resolve to Japan and its commitment to the residents and to the military. It is not an indicator of any resurgence in military importance of the islands.[143]

Although there may appear to be a military significance to the disputed islands, the author's assessment is that Russian claims to such are more rhetoric than reality and that military presence is meant as a method for communicating resolve to Japan and other foreign countries and to reassure its domestic constituency. The overall context is Russia's return to the status of a great power, and it is using its military to communicate that return to power, which is consistent historically. Russia's status as a great power has always been rooted in its identity as a military power. Economically, Russia was not able to afford its military prowess until the last decade of energy resource exports. With regard to the disputed islands, Russia's current concerns with its military facilities on Etorofu, access to the maritime straits, or ability to continue to utilize its sonar network are easily addressed either specifically in a peace treaty or in accompanying bi-lateral agreements.

Economic Cooperation: A Promising Future Remains Elusive

Economic cooperation between Russia and Japan includes both trade and investment. Trade at the commercial level consists of raw material exports from Russia to Japan, such as timber, and manufactured goods from Japan to Russia, such as consumer goods and automobiles. Russia has pursued a policy of seeking economic assistance from Japan. However, Japan has refrained from significant assistance at the national level. Since loans and investment are Japan's only means of leverage, Japan is refraining from significant assistance until the resolution of the territorial dispute.[144] Since Russia occupies the disputed islands, this is one of the few methods for Japan to exert any influence on Russia. Japanese leaders are reluctant to provide economic assistance prior to a resolution because they fear it will diminish their negotiating leverage. Furthermore, as Russia's economy improves with its oil wealth, economic assistance becomes less important than previously. It certainly is not as important to Russia today as it was during the Gorbachev and Yeltsin eras of the 80s and 90s. In 2007, Konstantin Sarkisov, a scholar on the disputed islands, described the diminished power of economic assistance as, "still attractive though not decisive."[145]

As the conflict continues to be entrenched, Japan risks losing potential market share to China and South Korea, particularly in energy resources and manufactured goods, respectively. For example, in 1992, Japan was the largest trading partner with the Sakhalin Oblast, which includes the Kurile archipelago. By 1999, South Korea supplanted Japan.[146]

It is unlikely that Japanese foreign investment has much to offer President elect Putin. Putin must carefully balance his traditionalist and paternalistic agenda with the increasing demands of the domestic population at large, in particular the educated. The

Russian protesters in the last six months are frustrated with the unfilled promises, injustice, corruption, dishonesty, and increasing disparity between the wealthy elite and the average citizen.[147] Economic assistance from the central Japanese government in the way of loans would probably do very little to help the average Russian citizen. Although the Russian economy is still fragile, Putin has more to gain by pursuing a strategy of independence and self sufficiency, especially given Russia's increased oil revenues. There is also the fear that Japanese loans would only line the pockets of Russia's elite, even if only indirectly.

Japanese business investment in Russia has not flourished for several reasons. Brad Williams' *Resolving the Russo-Japanese Territorial Dispute* provides a comprehensive assessment.[148] First, Japanese are wary of Russia's former communist elites who are now entrenched in the political, commercial, and criminal sectors. Second, Russian laws governing commercial practices are more quantitative than qualitative. They change frequently and are often inconsistent and even conflicting, especially between national and regional levels. Third, poor infrastructure, especially in the Russian Far East, does not create a consistent and reliable environment, such as shipping and communications, conducive for business investment. Fourth, complicated and redundant taxation systems reduce profit margins. Fifth, criminal activities and an absence of and disrespect for the rule of law impair trust and confidence and increase business risks. And sixth, a high level of negative publicity in both countries about joint business ventures exists. The most notable example is the Santa Resort Hotel joint business venture of the 90s. Disagreements over profit sharing ended up in litigation in the St. Petersburg Arbitration Court, which ruled in favor of the Russian enterprise and

31

took control of jointly held property. The Japanese business interest successfully appealed the decision to the Supreme Arbitration Court in Moscow.[149] However, the Japanese press succeeded in tainting public and commercial opinion by describing the incident as a Russian hi-jacking. Russian media incited domestic fears by describing the incident as a case of foreign exploitation and unscrupulous practices designed to take advantage of Russian business enterprises and even appealed to the need to protect Russia's national interests.

Williams further explains that despite the negative publicity surrounding joint ventures, they are often preferable to sole (Japanese) ownership, since they provide a Russian partner to help negotiate several of the challenges presented above. In addition, legal obstacles are often put in place to protect Russian commercial enterprises at the national and regional levels, in particular for construction contracts in support of energy projects.[150]

Despite the present situation characterized by a decrease in the importance of economic assistance to Russia, Japan's continued reluctance to provide substantial economic assistance, and a Russian business and investment climate that is not attractive to foreign investment,[151] one view of the future is that both countries could benefit from economic cooperation. Russia has resources, in particular energy (oil and natural gas), which Japan needs. Japan is highly dependent upon external resources for its energy and will increase its reliance on natural gas as it removes its nuclear power generation plants from service following the Fukushima Daiichi nuclear disaster in March, 2011.[152] Russia's needs extend far beyond the manufactured goods that it imports from Japan today. Russia could benefit substantially from Japanese management and technological expertise, particularly if Russia begins to shift from investing its oil wealth in its military to improving its infrastructure. Thus, Russo – Japanese economic cooperation will be a significant component for their future prosperity.

However, a less cooperative future is possible if the assessment of Nancy Birdsall and Francis Fukuyama proves accurate. They argue that to mitigate global economic competitiveness and volatility, emerging markets will prioritize policies that emphasize economic resilience over the flexibility and efficiency of the free market model.[153] They further portend that minimizing social disruption through state welfare and domestic industries will be more important than the free flow of capital and that emerging markets will be less inclined to utilize the intellectual expertise of foreign, developed countries. With the current high oil prices, which are likely to continue given the instability in the Middle East over concerns about Iran's suspected nuclear weapon development, Russia can generate sufficient revenues to pursue its national objectives. Furthermore, the recent, hard economic lessons that Iceland, Ireland, and Eastern Europe have endured due to the "foreign finance fetish"[154] are likely to be heeded in Russia.

Russia's quest for economic assistance included requests for support as it sought to join the Asia Pacific Economic Cooperation (APEC) forum in the 90s. Similarly, in the following decade (2000s), Russia sought Japan's support for its accession to the World Trade Organization (WTO). Both these goals have been accomplished, in November 1998 and December 2011, respectively. Overall, these are positive achievements, since they serve to bring Russia into the regional and global economic communities that enhance cooperation and support legal frameworks for interstate economic activities. In particular, APEC's Fisheries and Energy Working Groups could provide useful forums to expand cooperation in these areas, especially since South Korea and China are also members of APEC and have significant interests in fishing and energy. However, it must be noted that Russia's accession to both APEC and the WTO deprives Japan of two opportunities to provide Russia with cooperative support in the long term. In the short term, Japan has a limited time window to capitalize on its prior support of Russia's WTO membership.

Fishing and energy resources are of such economic importance that they are subsequently discussed in further depth. Fishing and marine processing are the primary commercial activities of the Russian residents on the disputed islands and a significant part of the local economies in Sakhalin and Hokkaido. Oil and natural gas exports from Russia to Japan are extremely important at the regional and national levels of both countries, since they are the primary revenue generators for Russia, and Japan is highly dependent upon foreign energy imports.

Local Economics: Fishing

The Kurile archipelago sits at the confluence of the cold Oyashio current from the north and the warm Kuroshio current from the south.[155] This creates nutrient rich waters that are the basis for one of the world's richest marine food chains. The Pacific Ocean waters to the southeast of the disputed islands are even more abundant than those of the Sea of Okhotsk.

The disputed islands are significant because they provide the territorial basis for maritime exclusive economic zones (EEZ), which are governed by the United Nations Convention on the Law of the Sea (UNCLOS). The EEZ establishes sovereignty over the primary economic interest of these waters, the fishing stocks.[156] Both Japan and Russia have signed and ratified UNCLOS.[157] The EEZ extends up to 200 nautical miles from shore, to the intersection of another sovereign nation's EEZ at their midpoint, or to a maritime delimitation by a formal instrument, such as a treaty. The Habomai islets, Kunashiri, and the southeast coast of Etorofu have EEZs that extend southeast into the Pacific Ocean. Shikotan and the northwest coast of Etorofu have EEZs that extend northeast into the Sea of Okhotsk. The EEZs to the southeast are larger. They extend to the full 200 nautical miles. The northwestern EEZs, in the Sea of Okhotsk, do not extend as far before they meet Sakhalin's EEZ extending southeastward. Russia has the fourth largest EEZ in the world, totaling 7,566,673 square kilometers. Japan ranks ninth with 4,479,358 square kilometers. The four disputed islands generate a maritime EEZ of 196,000 square kilometers, which account for 2.6% of Russia's or 4.4% of Japan's total EEZ.[158]

Fishing and marine food processing are well established industries in the Kuriles, Hokkaido, and Sakhalin. Fish and shellfish, including crabs, are exported from Russia, legally and illegally, and imported into Japan. In return, fishing nets and marine food packing materials are other manufactured goods are exchanged.[159] One of the manufactured goods is used cars, despite the difference in steering wheel configurations.[160] This trade has been described as "cars for crabs."[161]

Recent factors, such as the high cost of fuel and declining populations, have led to a decrease in both the Japanese and Russian fishing fleets. In addition, economic challenges in both countries have made work in other sectors more profitable and, therefore, more attractive. This situation encourages some in the fishing and seafood packing industries to change professions, even relocating if necessary, and discourages others, particularly the younger generations, from joining these industries. Despite the declines in the size of the fleets, fishing remains significant to the local economies in Russia and Japan, and therefore is a primary determinant of the interests in and opinions about the disputed islands at the local level.

Prior to 1977, both Japan and Russia fished relatively unencumbered. In 1977, Canada, the United States, Russia, Japan, and several other coastal nations extended their EEZ jurisdictions to 200 miles beyond their coastlines in an effort to protect endangered fish stocks.[162] Today, three principal documents signed in 1984, 1985, and 1998 define bi-lateral fishing agreements between Japan and Russia that permit fishing inside each other's EEZ using a quota (catch limits) and permit (fee) system.[163] The Japanese government at the national level carefully balances sustaining the local economy with the perception of tacit recognition of Russian sovereignty.[164] Thus, the Japanese government has de-emphasized these agreements at times.[165]

There are also arrangements for Russian vessels to dock directly in Japanese ports and sell their catch.[166] Parts of the proceeds are then immediately returned to the local economy as Russian sailors shop in Japanese stores; provision, outfit, and repair their fishing vessels; and eat, relax, and rest.[167] However, there are two challenges with this economic trade. First, exporting the catch directly to Japan does not sustain or promote any processing or packing industries in the Kuriles or Sakhalin, depriving these economies of desperately needed jobs and tax revenues.

Second, it is difficult for Russian fishing regulatory agencies to enforce Russian quotas on Russian vessels when the fish are caught and then directly off loaded in

Japan before the vessel returns to its Russian home port. Export and import customs reports in Russia and Japan for the trade of fish differ significantly, with the highest level of discrepancy in 1999, a difference of nine to one.[168] There is a significant illicit trade, of crabs and shellfish in particular, which garner the highest prices. Japanese officials at the local level often turn a blind eye to the Russian fish smuggling, since it provides additional seafood at cheap prices to Japan. Russian officials at the local level are often bribed with cash, alcohol, and seafood products for their acquiescence or for falsifying records.[169] Russian border guards have even been bribed to reveal the location and times of their patrols.[170] A counter-intuitive consequence of the illegal smuggling is a vicious circle: more seafood for sale, of crabs in particular, increases supply, decreasing the price and lowering profit margins for the fishermen, who then exceed their quotas and engage in illegal trade in order to maintain their overall income.[171]

The same vicious circle contributes to the Japanese fishing in the EEZ of the disputed islands, violating the bi-lateral agreements that permit fishing under specific conditions (locations, quantities, and fees). Russian officials consider this activity to be illegal poaching, while Japanese consider it to be perfectly legal fishing. To avoid Russian interference, many Japanese fishermen utilize high speed fishing vessels that allow them to evade Russian Border Guard vessels.[172]

The consequences of the Russian smuggling and Japanese poaching include lost revenues and unregulated over fishing that can have a detrimental effect on the stocks.[173] In an attempt to curb the illicit trade, Russian officials established customs posts in the disputed islands in the early and mid 90s.[174] Additionally, in 1993 Russia's border guards began enforcing poaching with use of force.[175] Between 1994 and 2005,

30 Japanese fishing vessels were detained, 210 crewmembers arrested, and seven injured, and in August 2006, a Japanese crewmember was killed.[176] Another step toward stemming the illicit trade was the 1998 bi-lateral fishing agreement, which was unique since it was the first agreement to specify the exact locations of agreed upon fishing, using reference points of latitude and longitude and their connecting geodesic lines.[177]

The net effect of the illicit fish trade has been to create a climate within which many local Russians and Japanese benefit and therefore do not want to see any change that would result from a territorial settlement. Polls indicate that there are Japanese who prioritize fishing rights over the actual land of the islands.[178] This is plausible, given that very few Japanese are still alive who actually lived on the islands, since they were deported immediately following World War II. There are also some Japanese who favor a two island solution (the transfer of Habomai and Shikotan), since these islands include the more abundant Pacific EEZ and would provide access that is not subject to Russian quotas or fees.[179] Finally, there are Russians who fear a settlement will disadvantage Russian fishermen due to an increase in fishing activity by the Japanese if the islands are returned to Japan.[180]

The local environments create two challenges at the national level. First, the frequent fishing incidents between Russia and Japan are highly publicized in the media, which perpetuates negative sentiments. Second, the differences between local and national interests deny either country, especially Japan, a unified and consistent approach to the dispute. In Japan, while fishing is an important local issue, it is not a primary consideration in resolving the dispute at the national level.[181] At the national level, Japan has had to engage local authorities in Hokkaido to clamp down on illegal poaching when action is demanded by Russia.[182] Furthermore, Japan has even resorted to "extra-budgetary" payments to Hokkaido in an attempt to alleviate the economic hardship on the Japanese fishermen and placate them into supporting the national objective of remaining steadfast on a four island solution.[183]

The overall result is that economic trade at the local level creates a hindrance to national level resolution.[184] In his book, *Resolving the Russo-Japanese Territorial Dispute: Hokkaido –Sakhalin Relations*, Brad Williams succinctly describes this tragedy,

> "Local trade was intended to bring the two regions closer together economically and make Sakhalin residents cognizant of the benefits of expanding such links, thereby alleviating their opposition to Russia transferring the disputed islands to Japan. Not only has it failed to do this, it has also had the unintended effect of creating and sustaining societal forces with a vested interest in continued Russian control over the South Kuril Islands, consisting of local fishers, the armed forces and law enforcement agencies."[185]

Any effort to enhance economic cooperation based on legal fishing and reduce the risk of maritime incidents between the two countries would be positive steps forward.[186] Illegal fishing interdictions can unnecessarily escalate from peaceful enforcement to forceful seizures. In addition, they are inflammatory and damaging to future cooperation and negotiations. Reducing the illicit trade (both smuggling and poaching) will require a synchronized response by authorities from both Russia and Japan and will need to be coordinated at both the national and local levels.[187] Cooperation in seafood harvesting, processing, packing, and storage and scientific and technological exchanges related to fisheries management are possible initiatives.[188] Vessel monitoring systems (VMS) with jointly monitored tracking could be extremely useful for both countries by enabling enforcement against smuggling and poaching.

These systems would also enable enforcement against poaching by fishermen of other countries, such as Korea and China. Unfortunately, a Russian proposal for this capability did not receive a favorable response from the Japanese.[189] Another possible cooperative measure is to allow Japanese officials on board Russian Border Guard patrol vessels and, in turn, to allow Russian customs officers to conduct their operations in Japanese ports in the three principal northern Hokkaido fishing towns of Wakkanai, Mombetsu, and Nemuro, where Russian vessels off load their catch.

In 2001, the South Korean government announced that it would begin fishing in the disputed waters, based on permission granted by the Russian government. Japan quickly protested this action.[190] As populations in South Korea and China rise and fish stocks decline, pressure to expand fishing areas will increase.[191] In the future, Russia could make any fishing concessions to other third party nations less provocative if the agreements were multi-lateral and included the Japanese; if any proceeds were directly spent on improving the fishing industry in the disputed waters, such as the previously discussed vessel monitoring systems; or if concessions were granted to both Russia and Japan for fishing rights in the third party's waters. Unfortunately, even the fees paid by Japanese fishermen under the quota-fee system have not reached the South Kurile district of the Sakhalin oblast, even when funds to rebuild infrastructure were desperately needed following the 1994 earthquake.[192]

Resolving the territorial dispute almost certainly will require a guarantee that Russia can retain its current fishing rights in the EEZ of the disputed islands.[193] Both Russian and Japanese fishermen will need to be reassured that their fishing concerns will be protected. The national level governments will need to agree to creative solutions that ensure both sides have more to gain from the resolution than they might lose. An interesting possibility mutually beneficial to Japan and Russia would be to prohibit both countries from granting any fishing concessions to any other third party nation.

To date, Japan has resisted any cooperative measures, to include Russian proposals for a free trade zone. Economic factors associated with the illicit trade, including Russian expenditures in Japanese ports and plentiful seafood at discounted illicit prices, are certainly one aspect of Japan's reticence.[194] The second is Japan's desire to remain steadfast in a demand for a four island solution. Japan is, in Kimura's assessment, convinced that any interim measure, such as a two island reversion with additional negotiations to follow, or economic concessions first as confidence building measures, will be stalled with a new status quo that is not likely to ever experience the follow on steps of resolution.[195] In other words, Japan is convinced that there will only be one negotiation. If one accepts this assumption, then Japan has only two choices, to remain steadfast to a four island solution as it has, even though the probability of resolution is low, or to accept a final solution that is less than four islands, with the risk that Russia will bargain in earnest once it becomes known that Japan has compromised its position.

Regional Economics: Oil and Gas

In contrast to the fishing industry, which is significant at the local level, energy resources are important at the national level.[196] The oil and natural gas extraction, transport, and export industries in the Russian Far East are strategically important to Japan, which is completely dependent upon imports. Economic cooperation in these areas is currently taking place and could have a positive impact on resolving the territorial dispute. In the event of a resolution, it is expected that Russo-Japanese

41

cooperation would further expand, benefitting both countries' energy sectors in terms of increased revenues for Russia and increased supply for Japan. Following the Fukushima Daiichi disaster, increased supply of natural gas is critical to Japan to support its electric power industry.[197] In addition, expansion of energy trade between the two countries diversifies their customers and suppliers,[198] which enhances stability of the energy sector, improves business ties, and promotes cooperation and understanding.

The Far East's energy potential is relatively undeveloped and therefore provides plenty of opportunity for cooperation. The East Siberia - Pacific Ocean (ESPO) pipeline will transport oil from fields in eastern Siberia to Russia's east coast for export to Asian markets.[199] The ESPO pipeline project comprises two phases, of which the first is complete. Oil exports to China were negotiated in 2009 under a 20 year agreement to provide 15 million tons per year (300,000 barrels per day) in exchange for US$25 billion in loans to the Russian oil companies Transneft and Rosneft for oil field and pipeline development.[200] Shipments began in January 2011. The second phase of the ESPO project is to continue the pipeline from Skovorodino to the port of Nakhodka at Kozmino Bay, located just east of Vladivostok. Depending upon the oil reserves in the east Siberian oil fields, it is expected to be operational in the 2015-2017 timeframe.[201] It is important to note that, although unlikely, there is a possibility that the east Siberian oil fields may not produce sufficient quantities to meet exports to both China and to the oil export facility at Nakhodka. If this proves true, Japan will not be able to diversify its oil imports and both Russia and Japan will not benefit from the resulting economic cooperation.

The Yakutia–Khabarovsk–Vladivostok pipeline project will allow export of natural gas from the Yakutia fields in Russia's Far East. Construction is scheduled to begin this year, with deliveries in 2016.

The Sakhalin II energy venture[202] is a positive example of cooperation that provides economic benefits at the regional level to the Sakhalin oblast. Japanese companies maintain a 22.5% stake in the consortium Sakhalin Energy. In addition to the development, extraction, and pipeline on the island of Sakhalin, the project also includes Russia's first liquid natural gas (LNG) plant, which became operational in 2009 and supports the export of natural gas via LNG tankers. Construction of the LNG plant was also a joint venture with Japanese engineering and construction firms. Additional financing of US$5.3 billion in 2008 included a loan from the Japan Bank for International Cooperation of US$3.7 billion. Today there are multiple long term (15 to 24 years) sales contracts to Japanese gas and electric power companies.[203] Benefits to the Sakhalin oblast include lower unemployment, vocational training, an improved tax base, and infrastructure upgrades in the areas of roads, ports, railways, telecommunications, hospitals, airports, and waste management.[204]

Gazprom's Sakhalin-Khabarovsk-Vladivostok pipeline, currently under construction, will transport Sakhalin's resources even further south, to the port of Nakhodka at Kozmino Bay, close to Vladivostok. This project includes an LNG production facility at its terminus for maritime LNG export. Nakhodka provides better year around maritime access than Prigorodnoye due to winter ice in the Sea of Okhotsk. Russia plans to provide substantial exports of both oil and LNG to the Asian market via Nakhodka.

Sakhalin III is a new project further off shore with currently unproven reserves that are being explored, with potential for production by 2020. The project provides Japanese companies with another investment opportunity that might prove helpful in resolving the territorial dispute. In order to reap positive benefits for resolution of the dispute, Japan should increase future investments and exploit current involvement in Russia's energy projects. One method for exploiting Japan's involvement would be to publicize, through the media, its participation in Russia's energy projects, in particular Sakhalin II, and the positive benefits to the local population. The intent would be to enhance opinions of the public and local and regional officials in Sakhalin, which currently are strongly opposed to any reversion of the disputed islands. Furthermore, Japan must recognize that its investments will have diminishing positive influence on the resolution of the territorial dispute as Russia's economy expands.

As Russia recognizes the importance of the Asian energy market and begins to increase its emphasis on its eastern markets, in contrast to its European markets, Japan has an opportunity to provide capital for Russia's Far East energy projects. Despite Russia's growing economy, it can still benefit from capital to finance new exploration, extraction, and transportation projects, and reinvest in the maintenance and upgrade of its existing, aging energy infrastructure. China is also postured to take advantage of the same opportunities and has a distinct advantage over Japan; China has a growing economy, large monetary reserves, and has resolved its territorial conflicts with Russia in 2004.

Cultural Identities: Similarities and Differences

Both Russia and Japan have very strong senses of identity. Nationalism has a long and strong history in both countries. However, both countries have different sources of power. Japan's source of power is economic, while Russia's is military might.[205] Familiarity with the similarities and differences in the cultural identities of Russia and Japan is helpful to understand their actions and the perceptions of those actions by the other party.

Japanese are respectful, adhere to protocol, and are steadfast in principles. They still have territorial disputes with South Korea and with China. Japan has consistently maintained its four island policy, which it immediately adopted following the 1951 San Francisco Peace Treaty and supports with a historical justification based on the 1855 Treaty of Shimoda. Russians interpret this behavior as inflexible and indicative of an unwillingness to compromise. The Japanese counter response is that they have been flexible, specifically in the timing, administration, and methodology of the reversion.

In contrast, Russians can be pragmatic and are able to bargain. They have resolved many of their territorial disputes in the last two decades, including with China in 2004. Throughout his historical dialogue, Kimura provides several observations of Russian negotiating behavior, including last minute changes, selectivity of parts of an agreement that he describes as "cherry picking" and a "bazaar" style negotiating technique of offers and counter offers and a resulting 50-50 split of the final difference.[206]

Japan and Russia have a significant difference in the way organizations function and how they formulate policy. Russians emphasize higher levels of authority. They have a top down methodology that upholds politics as supreme over all other matters. In contrast, Japanese develop ideas from below. They have a bottom up style that places priority on economics and legality as well as politics.[207] Therefore, lower level, sub-ministerial negotiations and working groups are beneficial to Japan but not to Russia. Additionally, in Japan it is more likely that regional and national agendas will be in harmony, whereas in Russia, it is possible that regional agendas may contrast with national level agendas.[208] An example of the former is the Hokkaido prefecture's cooperation with the Japanese national government directive to crack down on poachers' high speed fishing vessels. An example of the later is the strong personal stance of Governor Valentin Federov of the Sakhalin oblast in the 1990s. He proclaimed Russia's sovereignty over all four of the disputed islands, in contrast to Yeltsin's more conciliatory approach toward a resolution.

Richard D. Lewis provides important insights on various cultures in *When Cultures Collide: Leading Across Cultures*.[209] Russian[210] and Japanese[211] cultures are similar in some aspects, but for the most part contrast significantly. The implications of Lewis' observations are that confidence building measures can have success, both countries are very proud and therefore agreement is more likely if it does not embarrass or humiliate either side, and there is a strong propensity for stubbornness by both countries that can enable a stalemate. Areas of contrast between the cultures, that may provide challenges to a resolution, include differences in the nature of relationships and the use of language. Russians can leverage personal relationships, while Japanese must always seek consensus of their organization. In particular, Japan's frequent turnover of prime ministers makes it difficult to build a deep personal relationship with Putin. When communicating, Japanese are ambiguous and vague while Russians are direct and blunt. Russia should be aware that they must earn the trust and confidence of

Japan in order to be successful. Likewise, Japan must be willing to negotiate with Russia on a personal basis at the highest level.

Cultural sensitivity can have a profound effect on perceptions and media attention, which in turn can influence and insight domestic opinion. Russia's cancellation of summits, especially on short notice, certainly was not beneficial.[212] In contrast, Russia's apology for the long detention of Japanese prisoners of war was a positive step.[213]

Finally, both sides should remember that a resolution is most likely to occur when the leaders are at the peak of their domestic credibility. Any resolution will be unpopular with at least some of the domestic populations. The timing of a resolution will need to capitalize on a leader's domestic popularity. Kimura attributes mistiming as contributing to the failure of negotiations under both Gorbachev and Yeltsin.[214]

Resident Population

Russian residents may have succeeded in changing Russian policy on development in the islands. Their discontent with the neglect by the Russian government could have led to their recent interest in the islands. The residents were appreciative of the Japanese assistance provided to the islands after the 1994 earthquake, especially in light of the minimal response from the Russian government.[215] They expressed their gratitude for Japanese assistance and their displeasure with their own government, which was reported in the media.[216] In 2009, Russia thanked Japan for the humanitarian assistance it has been providing to the four disputed islands since the 1994 earthquake, stating that the aid was no longer necessary.[217] Following President Medvedev's visit to the islands in 2010, Russia promised more than US$1 billion in social economic development of the islands through 2015.[218] The assistance will support new roads and airports, new houses, geothermal energy, deep water ports, and a seafood processing industry.

Framework for a Possible Resolution

Kimura describes the dispute as deadlocked due to an inability of both sides to compromise. He acknowledges that Japan has not changed its position on the reversion of all four islands.[219] Kimura provides the same assessment of Russia, "It is also a fact that the Russian side has not moved at all from the 'return of only two islands' formula that the Soviet Union stated under Khrushchev more than half a century ago."[220] Without compromise, these two positions are irreconcilable.

Kimura's position is that Japan has shown flexibility. He cites two reasons. First, in the 1951 San Francisco Peace Treaty, Japan renounced its claim to the central and northern Kurile Islands and to the southern half of Sakhalin.[221] In addition, Kimura points out that Japan officially stated in 1992, "Tokyo will be flexible over the timing, modalities, and conditions of the return of the islands."[222]

In contrast to Kimura's assessment of Russian inflexibility is a statement by Putin in 2006. When questioned about the territorial dispute with Japan at a meeting, Putin indicated a flexible foreign policy. His response described Russia's resolution of its territorial disputes with China, "We took steps toward each other and undertook mutual compromises, acceptable to the Chinese as well as to us, and that's because each side really wanted to close this page in our relations and create a basis for long-term good-neighborly relations – and we did it."[223] This response and the resolution of several other territorial disputes during his first presidential tenure demonstrate that Putin understands the importance of compromise and can adopt a pragmatic approach toward a resolution.[224]

Furthermore, Konstantin Sarkisov, a noted scholar of Russian – Japanese relations, concludes that "two and two" and "two plus alpha" proposals demonstrate some creativity of Russian leaders in trying to find an acceptable resolution.[225] The two and two proposal treats Habomai and Shikotan as distinct from Kunashiri and Etorofu, with both issues being negotiated in parallel, simultaneously but separately.[226] The two and two proposal has never been officially confirmed.[227] The two plus alpha proposal sought a solution that included the reversion of Habomai and Shikotan to Japan, plus some other, undetermined measures, described as "alpha."[228] This proposal originated after Putin's 2004 reelection. However, these solutions did not prove acceptable, due to Japanese suspicions that a final solution would never be forthcoming.[229]

In 2002, Japan fired several of its senior foreign ministry bureaucrats for their apparent willingness to compromise on the steadfast Japanese policy of four island reversion.[230] Sarkisov provides the following critique, "Finding a compromise requires taking a risk, and after the severe punishment of those who had done so no one was prepared to risk the same fate by following their example."[231] Thus, he came to the conclusion that the inability to compromise will perpetuate the stalemate.[232]

Kimie Hara assesses that compromise is unlikely since the Japanese four island solution "has become solidified as a domestic policy norm."[233] With a weak central government and a culture that emphasizes loyalty and the collective whole, it is unlikely that Japan's government is strong enough to agree to a territorial compromise, which would be contrary to the strong domestic irredentist movement in Hokkaido. Therefore, Hara argues that bi-lateral attempts at resolution have been and will remain deadlocked if attempts at resolution remain in a bi-lateral framework.[234] She offers a multi-lateral framework for negotiation as the best opportunity for success.[235] Hara's multi-lateral

proposal has its origins in a 2006 international conference on the disputed islands that

was held in Åland, Finland, and specifically analyzed the 1921 Åland resolution for

possible inspiration in the Russo-Japanese dispute.[236] Hara proposes that a multi-lateral

forum may provide a framework "without loss of face" for Russia and Japan.[237] She

offers the International Court of Justice (ICJ)[238] or the nations of the Six Party Talks[239] as

possible forums. Another expert recommends the Organization of Security and

Cooperation in Europe (OSCE), of which Russia is a member and Japan an observer,

as a possible forum.[240]

Hara provides two additional suggestions for resolution framework. First, she

proposes a comprehensive approach of "creatively combining conditions" that might

include "political, economic, military, or non-conventional security agendas of the

concerned states."[241] Second, she offers an approach that links several other disputes in

a multi-lateral framework, such as the territorial disputes between Japan and South

Korea, Japan and China, and the South China Sea islands.[242] A comprehensive

approach is certainly warranted. In addition to considering the rights of the residents,

militarization, and economic factors of the islands' EEZ, an agreement could include

other economic agreements, or military concessions.[243] However, the proposal of a

multi-dimensional agreement of several disputes in a multi-lateral framework is ideal but

appears unrealistic due to being overly complicated and prone to be very time

consuming.

Markku Heiskanen draws insights from the Åland resolution for autonomy,

demilitarization, neutralization, and guarantees of minority rights, but provides a

50

contrary opinion on the benefits of a multi-lateral forum.[244] He states, "The dispute must be resolved between Japan and Russia only. It is not imaginable that the issue could be handled at the United Nations, the ICJ or any other international forum."[245] It is not likely that either side would be willing to accept the risk of an unfavorable solution imposed by a multi-lateral forum. This is especially true of Japan, which does not benefit from a culture or climate of successful multi-lateral organizations in Asia. Japan relations with its Asian neighbors can be described as cordial and cooperative, but not of mutual trust and confidence, a consequence of Japan's harsh colonization and occupation during World War II. Therefore, a bi-lateral solution must be found that allows for both sides to minimize their embarrassment.

There are various alternative solutions that are not viable due to reasons of feasibility, acceptability, or suitability. Independent sovereignty is not feasible since the four islands do not have the capacity for governance as a nation state. Joint sovereignty would require both Japan and Russia to relinquish their claims and provokes additional matters of concern, such as jurisdiction and taxation; thus, it is impractical.[246] In addition, the joint sovereignty of Sakhalin from 1855 to 1875 was not successful.[247] Territorial sovereignty could be suspended, as it is with Antarctica.[248] However, this only postpones a final resolution and is likely to provide a source for future conflict since bi-lateral arrangements are not always durable.[249] The Soviet Union's renunciation of the Neutrality Pact is a historical example that makes either joint sovereignty or the suspension of sovereignty undesirable for Japan. At least one author has proposed a world park as a possible solution.[250] The only advantage that this solution offers to Japan and Russia is a sacrifice of their interests for a higher cause. However, the sacrifices for both countries are significant. Domestic pressures from Hokkaido's irredentists and the Russian residents of the islands would most likely prohibit this noble but unsuitable proposal.

Åland's resolution provides four very relevant considerations for any negotiation of the disputed islands. These are autonomy, demilitarization, neutralization, and guarantees of rights for the residents. Autonomy is a possible option, and the most likely one if Japan obtains sovereignty. Permanent demilitarization and guarantees of neutralization could address the concerns of the conservative Russian military. The residents' would certainly need guarantees of property rights and citizenship, as well as other cultural concerns such as language.

Confidence building measures may prove beneficial for improving relations between the two countries and alleviating domestic concerns. These measures could be sequential and incremental in nature in the areas of joint economic development,[251] cooperation in humanitarian areas, and customs, fishery, and law enforcement. Possible humanitarian measures include medical exchanges, earthquake and tsunami warning and response, maritime search and rescue operations, disaster relief, and continuation of the visa free visits that have been occurring since 1992. Measures could be established to reduce the impact of high level visits to the islands, which incite the domestic populations in Sakhalin and Hokkaido.

Hara provides a different assessment of confidence building measures. She states that those who propose confidence building measures as a pre-condition to a resolution are only postponing an agreement.[252] Sarkisov presents his opinion that despite the rhetoric from Russian leaders about the need for strengthening multi-lateral ties between the two countries, there is no significant shift in the Russian position.[253] Finally, it appears that confidence building measures are actually regressing. Russia terminated Japanese humanitarian assistance in 2009. Japan declined President Medvedev's offer to create a free enterprise zone in 2010. And Russia began increasing its military presence on the islands in 2011. Thus, it is reasonable to conclude that both Japan and Russia, at the national level, are frustrated with the inability to reach an agreement. However, neither side is able to positively influence its domestic populace, and Japan's steadfast insistence on a four island reversion prevents any contributions of Russian pragmatism. Instead, Russia is acting as can be expected. According to Lewis, Russians will "rebel if they feel the pressure is intolerable." [254] This would explain the start of their military modernization initiative in 2011.

Recommendation: A Three Island Solution

A three island solution may be the best proposal.[255] This solution is sometimes referred to as "50-50 split,"[256] following the logic that Russia has already agreed to the reversion of Shikotan and Habomai in the 1956 Joint Declaration. That leaves the islands of Kunashiri and Etorufu to be divided as a compromise. The solution is feasible. Presently the island of Etorofu is part of the Kurilsky administrative district whereas the islands of Kunashiri, Shikotan, and Habomai comprise the Yuzhno-Kurilsky district.

Both countries may be able to accept this solution, since it is a compromise that does not seem to favor either side over the other. Thus, it could minimize the embarrassment to both, if they emphasized the gains of the resolution and downplayed the losses. It also provides an EEZ to both countries that includes Pacific waters to the southeast as well as waters in the Sea of Okhotsk to the northwest.

Perhaps most significant, the idea was suggested indirectly and was not met with outright disapproval. In September 2006, Japanese Foreign Minister Tarō Aso made the suggestion in an interview that was published in a Japanese newspaper. In November 2006, Putin and Japanese Prime Minister Shinzō Abe met briefly at the APEC summit in Hanoi and agreed to intensify their efforts. However, when questioned on the proposal during a debate in the Commission for Foreign Affairs of the Japanese parliament in December, Aso denied the proposal. Most interesting is the silent response in Russia. A few weeks later, the Russian Chairman of the Upper House International Committee of the Duma published an article with the following,

> "Russia's foreign policy in recent times is distinguished by pragmatism. … What about taking a risk, abandoning for the time being the generally correct principle of 'not an inch of the homeland' and turn the question of the four islands into a judgment about what these islands give us in political and economic terms."[257]

Unfortunately the proposal never solidified. However, it does appear that at that time, it would have been palatable to Russia.

A three island solution appears suitable as well. It provides a distinct border between the two countries at the significant strait and provides Japan with Kunashiri, which is very close to Hokkaido. A three island solution would enable Russian residents to move from Kunashiri or Shikotan to Etorofu. Finally, the most significant resident population and Russian military facilities are on the island of Etorofu and would not be disrupted by a three island solution.

Finally, a question, if all goes well, that will need to be answered in the near future is how to implement the legal aspects of a bi-lateral agreement between Japan and Russia. Is a peace treaty between the two nations sufficient for the international community or should the San Francisco Treaty be amended and signed by the 48 original signatories? Another possibility is for Russia to accede to the San Francisco Treaty.

<u>Risks and Time</u>

An often cited risk for Russia is a precedent that other territories ceded as a result of World War II might demand a change in status.[258] Kimura provides a cursory review of the possibilities of opening "Pandora's box" and concludes that this is not a significant risk.[259] Karelia is a possible exception.[260] There is also some sensitivity of the Russian Navy with respect to Kaliningrad, since it is the only ice free port for the Baltic Fleet.[261] However, there are no movements within Finland or Germany for the return of Karelia or Kaliningrad at this time.[262]

Currently, the sovereignty of the entire Kurile archipelago and to a lesser extent, Sakhalin Island, is in question.[263] Japan renounced its claims in the San Francisco Peace Treaty, but the question to whom remains unanswered, since it wasn't specified in the treaty and the Soviet Union was not a signatory. Sakhalin's sovereignty is slightly less open ended, since the San Francisco Peace Treaty renounces Japan's claim to territory it ceded as a result of the 1905 Treaty of Portsmouth, to which Russia was a signatory. Thus, the literal status of the Kurile archipelago and Sakhalin could be interpreted as "international" at this time. Although a counter claim by any other nation on the physical land is unlikely, it is possible that the EEZs, territorial waters, or the airspace associated with these areas could be contested.

Another risk is confrontation[264] that might escalate, purposely or accidentally, to conflict.[265] Confrontations occur fairly regularly due to the fishing fleets and the Japanese poachers. In 2006, confrontation resulted in the death of one Japanese fisherman.[266]

An interesting byproduct of a successful negotiation could be that Japan receives the three islands, and after some period of time, the Russian residents have migrated, either willingly or under the terms of resolution. What would Japan intend to do with the islands? Would it bring infrastructure and development to such a remote location? If not, it could be the subject of criticism of negotiating for the islands with no interest other than the principle of its sovereignty and the EEZ for its fishing fleet based in Hokkaido. Russia's domestic population, especially in Sakhalin, could argue that Russian residents were adversely impacted for no apparent reason. Thus, Japan needs to consider the amount of investment that it will take to help substantiate a legitimate interest in the islands. This has probably factored into Japan's reassurances to the Russian residents that they will be able to remain on the islands if they desire and the promise of development. The only alternative that Japan could possibly navigate would be to declare the islands as a national park or sanctuary.

The passage of time is important to consider. The conflict has lasted for 65 years, and a resolution does not appear to be in sight. Russia's de facto occupation of the islands becomes more normal and acceptable with each passing day. The Japanese irredentists based in Hokkaido consist of a small core of the former 17,300 Japanese residents of the disputed islands who were forcibly repatriated by the Soviet Union in 1946. This population is aging and dying.[267] Additionally, many of the people present during the early negotiations have died.[268] The passage of time does not favor Japan.[269] Japan must decide if it wants to remain steadfast to its principles and therefore remain in a stalemate forever, or if it can sacrifice some pride to regain part of its territory. If Japan desires a resolution, it is in their best interest to settle as early as possible.

For Russia, an earlier settlement is in its best interest as well, in order to achieve normal relations with Japan. However, the status quo is not a significant problem for Russia. Japan's steadfast position affects the government and economic assistance at the federal level. However, it does not prevent interaction at the commercial level. It is unlikely that Japan would prevent commercial exports to Russia, of cars for example. Furthermore, as Japan's energy resource requirements grow, its commercial cooperation with Russia becomes increasingly more important. Thus, although Russia does not benefit from fully normal relations with Japan, the lack of these relations is more of a nuisance than a significant hindrance.

Russia is certainly aware that time is on its side. In February 2007, while visiting Tokyo, Russian Prime Minister Mikhail Fradkov stated, "This issue needs to be tackled in no hurry, instead letting our cooperation develop, primarily in the trade and economic time. It will evidently take time."[270] More recently, a Russian foreign policy expert commented after Medvedev's November 2010 visit to the islands, "We've said many times that we're ready to return those two islands in exchange for normalizing relations, but for Russia it's absolutely not urgent."[271]

Conclusion

A three island solution offers the best possibility of a resolution to the territorial dispute between Japan and Russia over the four islands of Etorofu, Kunashiri, Shikotan, and the Habomai islets. The three island solution is a compromise that is feasible and suitable, and has the best chance of acceptability by both countries.

As the United States focuses on the Asia Pacific region, it should recognize the importance to regional stability that fully normal relations between Russia and Japan, via a peace treaty, could provide. The United States should emphasize the benefits of a resolution to Russia and Japan and offer to provide assistance in negotiations in whatever capacity both countries desire. As the primary architect of the San Francisco Peace Treaty, the United States has precedence for involvement in the resolution of the territorial dispute.

Perhaps the best opportunity for a renewed effort is the upcoming 2012 Summit of the Asia Pacific Economic Cooperation forum in Vladivostok in September. Japan could initiate a renewed bi-lateral effort by voicing its interest in a resolution and its willingness to consider a three island compromise. Alternatively, the United States could initiate a tri-lateral dialogue. The 2012 APEC summit would coincide with a time when President Putin's power is likely to be at its highest, and therefore may be willing to accept a domestically unpopular, compromise solution.

However, culture and the political and economic climates in both countries have prevented a resolution. These conditions are not likely to change in the foreseeable future. Therefore, the dispute will remain deadlocked.[272]

Nationalism is a very powerful cultural aspect in both countries. Change within the domestic political climate of Russia and Japan would enable the central governments to undertake the necessary compromises in their two island and four island policies, respectively. However, this change is unlikely. Economic and humanitarian confidence building measures over the last twenty years have been unsuccessful in changing public opinion substantially.

The Japanese Parliament and the Tokyo Ministry of Foreign Affairs are loyal to the irredentist movement in Hokkaido.[273] Furthermore, Japanese Prime Ministers are not strong enough to lead any change in foreign policy. The Hokkaido fishermen and local commercial interests benefit economically from the current deadlocked situation through poaching and trade with Russian fishermen.

Likewise, in Russia, the Sakhalin fishermen and the Russian border guards and fisheries officials benefit economically from the current stalemate by black market smuggling and bribes. At the national level, the conservative military continues to misrepresent the islands as a vital strategic interest. However, President Putin does possess the power and pragmatism to drive foreign policy in the direction of his choosing.

Currently, there are not any factors at the national level that are significant enough to create a desire to achieve fully normal relations between Japan and Russia. Economic cooperation is occurring through commercial investment and trade. This trade is vital to Japan, particularly in the area of energy resources. Therefore, Japan is unlikely to prohibit their industries from engaging in trade. Furthermore, as Russia's economy grows due to its energy exports, its need for significant financial assistance in the form of Japanese investment (federal loans) is decreasing.

Both countries are frustrated with the current situation. Compromise is less likely during periods of higher tension. Both sides are adhering to policies that are irreconcilable without compromise. Although Russia has the ability to compromise, Japan must garner the will to be more flexible. This is unlikely, and therefore the dispute will remain deadlocked for the foreseeable future until an outside factor is significant

enough to make fully normal relations worthy of a compromise.

This dispute provided a good case study of the influences of culture, domestic

politics, and economics on foreign policy. The history of the conflict also provided

several learning points, including the pitfalls of vague language in formal agreements

and the consequences of unintended communications.[274]

Endnotes

[1] The author preferred to use the Russian collective name, Southern Kuriles, in the title of the paper, because it is geographically more specific and descriptive and more widely recognized, than the Japanese collective name, Northern Territories (Japanese: Hoppo Ryodo), for the four disputed islands. The Japanese names for the four islands are Etorofu, Kunashiri, Shikotan, and Habomai shoto. The Russian names are Iturup, Kunashir, Shikotan, and Malaia Kurilskaia griada (which includes Shikotan), respectively. In English, Habomai shoto is also referred to as Habomai Islets or Habomai Rocks, since it is a collection of several lesser islets and rocks. Most of the Kurile Archipelago is made up of the Greater Kurile Ridge islands. However, the archipelago might include the Lesser Kurile Ridge islands, which consists of the island of Shikotan and the group of islets and rocks known as Habomai. Looking at Figure 1, one can see the distinction. The Lesser Kurile Ridge appears as an extension of the island of Hokkaido, whereas the Greater Kurile Ridge is the long archipelago that stretches to Kamchatka. Significant confusion has persisted by various uses of geographic, geologic, and political references. Essentially, 1) did the term "Kurile Islands" refer to the Lesser Kurile Ridge also, or only to the Greater Kurile Ridge, and 2) did the term "Kurile Islands" refer to the entire Greater Kurile Ridge archipelago, or did it exclude the islands that have always been under Japanese jurisdiction, specifically Kunashiri and Shikotan and the Lesser Kurile Ridge. This confusion is at the center of the territorial dispute. For the body of the paper, the author uses either the disputed islands or the more politically descriptive term of Northern Territories, since it specifically refers to the Lesser Kurile Ridge islands (Habomai and Shikotan) and the two Greater Kurile Ridge islands of Kunashiri and Etorofu, and which Japan has consistently stated are in dispute since 1945. The Soviet Union has presented different positions with respect to the dispute at different times in the last 65 years. At this time, Russia does acknowledge all four islands are in dispute.

[2] The four islands of Etorofu, Kunashiri, Shikotan, and Habomai shoto are 3184, 1499, 253, and 100 square kilometers in size, respectively.

[3] The Soviet Union seized the islands between August 28th and September 5th, 1945.

[4] The divisional lines of 1855 and 1875 are formal demarcations, as agreed to by the Treaties of Shimoda and St. Petersburg, respectively. The divisional line of 1945 represents the extension of the area administered by the Soviet Union (then, now the Russian Federation). It is

precisely the difference between the lines of 1855 and 1945 that make up the islands disputed by the two countries. Japan refers to this area as the Northern Territories. Russia refers to them as the Southern Kuriles. For the source of the figure, see Kimie Hara, "Untying the Kurillian Knot: Toward an Åland-Inspired Solution for the Russo-Japanese Territorial Dispute", *The Asia-Pacific Journal*, Vol. 24-2-09, June 15, 2009, http://japanfocus.org/-Kimie-HARA/3170 (accessed February 1, 2012).

[5] Rich in both diversity and abundance.

[6] Additional Japanese territorial disputes include: 1) Takeshima / Dokdo Islands: Japan – South Korea, 2) Senkaku / Diaoyu Islands: Japan – China - Taiwan, and 3) Okinotorishima: Japan and China. There are also disputes in the South China Sea, most notably 1) the Paracel Islands: Vietnam, China, and Taiwan, and 2) the Spratly Islands: Vietnam, China, Taiwan, Malaysia, Philippines, and Brunei.

[7] John J. Stephan, *The Kuril Islands: Russo-Japanese Frontiers in the Pacific* (Oxford, UK: Clarendon Press, 1974).

[8] Another in depth account is John A. Harrison, *Japan's Northern Frontier: A Preliminary Study in Colonization and Expansion with Special Reference to the Relations of Japan and Russia* (Gainesville, FL: University of Florida Press, 1953).

[9] Hiroshi Kimura, *The Kurillian Knot: A History of Japanese-Russian Border Negotiations* (Stanford, CA: Stanford University Press, 2008).

[10] In 1992, the Ministries of Foreign Affairs of Japan and the Russian Federation compiled the first edition of the *Joint Compendium of Documents on the History of Territorial Issue between Japan and Russia*, comprised of a preface and 35 documents. In 2001, the Ministries agreed to the new edition of the *Joint Compendium*, adding another preface and 7 additional documents. Linked from the *Ministry of Foreign Affairs of Japan Home Page*, http://www.mofa.go.jp/region/europe/russia/territory/index.html (accessed January 13, 2012).

[11] Kimura, *The Kurillian Knot*, 21-22.

[12] Ministry of Foreign Affairs of Japan and Ministry of Foreign Affairs of the Russian Federation, *Joint Compendium of Documents on the History of Territorial Issue between Japan and Russia,* First Edition (1992), linked from the *Ministry of Foreign Affairs of Japan Home Page*, http://www.mofa.go.jp/region/europe/russia/territory/edition92/index.html (accessed January 13, 2012). Subsequently referred to as *Joint Compendium*.

[13] Officially titled the Treaty of Commerce, Navigation, and Delimitation Between Japan and Russia of February 7, 1855. See Kimura, *The Kurillian Knot*, 26-27, Also see *Joint Compendium* http://www.mofa.go.jp/region/europe/russia/territory/edition92/index.html (accessed January 13, 2012).

[14] Kimura, *The Kurillian Knot*, 30-31. Also see *Joint Compendium*, http://www.mofa.go.jp/region/europe/russia/territory/edition92/index.html (accessed January 13, 2012).

[15] The negotiations were successful for both sides. Japan succeeded in having Russia withdraw militarily from Manchuria and Korea, which was important because Japan had reached the limit of its military and financial resources. Russia succeeded in not paying any war reparations to Japan, and retaining half of Sakhalin, despite the fact that it was occupied entirely by Japan during the war. The treaty was mediated by President Roosevelt, for which he won the Nobel Peace Prize. The treaty states, "The Imperial Russian Government shall cede to the Imperial Government of Japan, in perpetuity and full sovereignty, the southern portion of the island of Sakhalin, and all the islands adjacent thereto, as well as all the public works and properties there situated. The fiftieth degree of north latitude shall be adopted as the northern boundary of the ceded territory." See Kimura, *The Kurillian Knot*, 35. Also see *Joint Compendium*, http://www.mofa.go.jp/region/europe/russia/territory/edition92/index.html (accessed January 13, 2012).

[16] Officially titled the Convention Embodying Basic Rules of the Relations Between Japan and the Union of Soviet Socialist Republics, on January 20, 1925. Also referred to as the Peking Convention or the Soviet – Japanese Basic Convention. It also pledged to reexamine all other treaties signed before November 7, 1917 at a future conference. Finally, there was a Soviet Declaration that denied any political responsibility for the Treaty of Portsmouth, which it placed on the former Tsarist Government which signed it. See Kimura, *The Kurillian Knot*, 38. Also see *Joint Compendium*, http://www.mofa.go.jp/region/europe/russia/territory/edition92/index.html (accessed January 13, 2012).

[17] In 1940, Japan began to seek a nonaggression pact with the USSR. However, the Soviet Union demanded the return of the southern half of Sakhalin and the Kurile Islands, otherwise it would only sign a neutrality pact. There is some dispute about the exact definition of the Kurile Islands; possible interpretations are either the northern islands as described in the Treaty of St. Petersburg or all the Kurile Islands, to include some or all of those previously agreed as Japanese in the Treaty of Shimoda. Kimura presents a compelling argument for the former, using a source with firsthand knowledge of the initial negotiations on April 7, 1941 and the precedence of the St. Petersburg Treaty. Kimura came to the conclusion that there was no intentional ambiguity and that the Soviet reference was specific to only the northern Kurile Islands. See Kimura, *The Kurillian Knot*, 40. Also see *Joint Compendium*, http://www.mofa.go.jp/region/europe/russia/territory/edition92/index.html (accessed January 13, 2012).

[18] The first two of eight principles state, "First, their countries seek no aggrandizement, territorial or other; Second, they desire to see no territorial changes that do not accord with the freely expressed wishes of the peoples concerned…" On September 24, 1941, the Soviet Government acceded to the Atlantic Charter by declaration. It stated, "…the Soviet Government expresses its agreement with the basic principles of the declaration of the President of the United States Mr. Roosevelt and the Prime Minister of Great Britain Mr. Churchill and main principles that are of great importance in the current international situation." See *Joint Compendium*, http://www.mofa.go.jp/region/europe/russia/territory/edition92/index.html (accessed January 13, 2012).

[19] Ibid.

[20] The northern Kuriles were ceded to Japan in 1875 by the Treaty of St. Petersburg. Thus, the entire Kuriles are not subject to the Cairo Declaration. In addition, Sakhalin was first occupied in its entirety by the Japanese during the Russo – Japanese War in 1905. The Treaty

of Portsmouth followed, which negotiated the division of the island at the 50th parallel. Similar actions occurred in 1920-1925, occupation by force followed by a treaty. Thus, with respect to the Cairo Declaration, the status of the southern half of Sakhalin is open to interpretation, depending upon one's emphasis on occupation by violence or peaceful resolution by treaty. See Kimura, *The Kurillian Knot*, 42-43.

[21] In early February 1945, the Allied Powers held a summit at Yalta to discuss their vision of the post war world. On February 8, Roosevelt and Stalin met and discussed the Soviet Union's entry into the war against Japan, which Stalin had been considering for at least a year. The United States was anxious for the Soviet Union to enter the war against Japan to alleviate U.S. casualties. Stalin articulated his desire for southern Sakhalin and the Kurile Islands, which Roosevelt accepted. This dialogue is documented in the *Joint Compendium*. As evidenced by the Pacific War Council of January 12, 1944, during which Stalin expressed his desire for the return of all of Sakhalin and to have the Kurile Islands. Furthermore, in October, 1944 Stalin indicated to the US Ambassador to the Soviet Union that the Kurile Islands and lower Sakhalin should be returned in order for the Soviet Union to enter the war against Japan. The Ambassador communicated this information in a telegram to President Roosevelt on December 15, 1944. There is some discussion that Roosevelt probably was not aware of the status of the southern Kurile Islands, as determined by the Treaty of Shimoda in 1855, and that he assumed they were seized in the Russo – Japanese war of 1904 – 1905. Kimura cites a source that states a scholarly paper was prepared for Roosevelt to read before his meeting with Stalin, which emphasized that Japan had legally and peacefully acquired the southern Kurile Islands by treaty and should retain them. There is no evidence that Roosevelt read the paper. Kimura comes to the conclusion that even if he had, Roosevelt probably would have still acquiesced to Stalin's request, in order to obtain the Soviet Union's entry into the war against Japan and therefore minimize American casualties. There is a slight difference in the exact understanding of the conversation between Stalin and Roosevelt. Both are indicated in the *Joint Compendium*. The U.S. historical record states, "...Marshall Stalin said that he would like to discuss the political conditions under which the USSR would enter the war against Japan. He said he had already had a conversation on this subject with Ambassador Harriman. The President said he had received a report of this conversation, and he felt that there would be no difficulty whatsoever in regard to the southern half of Sakhalin and the Kurile Islands going to Russia at the end of the war..." The Soviet record states, "Stalin said that he would like to know the status of the political conditions under which the USSR would enter the war against Japan. An exchange took place regarding the political questions which he, Stalin, had already discussed with Harriman in Moscow. Roosevelt answered that the southern part of Sakhalin and the Kurile Islands would be handed over the Soviet Union." See Kimura, *The Kurillian Knot*, 43-45. Also see *Joint Compendium*,
http://www.mofa.go.jp/region/europe/russia/territory/edition92/index.html (accessed January 13, 2012).

[22] *Joint Compendium*,
http://www.mofa.go.jp/region/europe/russia/territory/edition92/index.html (accessed January 13, 2012).

[23] It is interesting to note that at the time of the compilation of the Joint Compendium in 1992, the Russian position de-emphasized the Yalta Agreement, which previously the Soviet Union had upheld as their primary justification for their position. See Kimura, *The Kurillian Knot*, 46-48.

[24] *Joint Compendium,*
http://www.mofa.go.jp/region/europe/russia/territory/edition92/index.html (accessed January 13, 2012).

[25] Acting in accordance with the pact, the Soviet Union decided to not renew the Pact at the end of its initial five year term. It became effective on April 13, 1941, and required either party to notify the other of their intent to not renew the Pact at least one year prior to its expiration. Thus, the Soviet denunciation conformed to the Pact.

[26] The Potsdam Declaration upheld the Cairo Declaration, to which the Kuriles in their entirety are not subject, as one of the conditions of surrender. However, it created some ambiguity when it stated, "8. The terms of the Cairo Declaration shall be carried out and Japanese sovereignty shall be limited to the islands of Honshu, Hokkaido, Kyushu, Shikoku and such minor islands as we determine." The wording "minor islands" is subject to interpretation. Additionally, it is possible to interpret the words "as we determine" as open ended. In accordance with international law, this would be the proper determination, since only a treaty and not a declaration, can establish sovereignty. The Potsdam Declaration also included this term, "7. Until such a new order is established and until there is convincing proof that Japan's war-making power is destroyed, points in Japanese territory to be designated by the Allies shall be occupied to secure the achievement of the basic objectives we are here setting forth." This established the authority for occupation after the War. See the Joint Compendium, http://www.mofa.go.jp/region/europe/russia/territory/edition92/index.html (accessed January 13, 2012).

[27] It is interesting to note that at the time of the declaration of war, the Neutrality Pact was still in effect between the two countries. Although the Soviet Union denounced the Neutrality Pact on April 5, 1945, the Pact was still valid for its full five year term, from its signing on April 13, 1941. Thus, the Soviet Union declared war while the Pact was still valid. It appears that the Soviet Union wanted, at least in part, to meet its obligation to the allies to enter the war against Japan within two to three months of the end of the war in Europe, which was part of the Yalta Agreement. The German surrender on May 7, 1945 became effective on the following day. Thus, the Soviet Union met its obligation to its allies of the Yalta Agreement by violating the Neutrality Pact with Japan. The preface to the first edition of the Joint Compendium describes this fact as follows, "In the Neutrality Pact between Japan and the USSR of April 13, 1941, the parties had an obligation to mutually respect each other's territorial integrity and inviolability. The Pact also stated that it would remain in force for five years and that if neither of the contracting parties denounced it a year before its date of expiration, it be considered to be automatically extended for the next five years. After the Soviet Union announced its intention to denounce the Japanese-Soviet Neutrality Pact on April 5, 1945, the Pact was to have become invalid on April 25, 1946. The Soviet Union declared war on Japan on August 9, 1945." See Kimura, *The Kurillian Knot*, 48-49. Also see the Joint Compendium, http://www.mofa.go.jp/region/europe/russia/territory/edition92/index.html (accessed January 13, 2012).

[28] Kimura explains how this information came to light by a Russian researcher in 1992. See Kimura, *The Kurillian Knot*, 49-51.

[29] Ibid, 51.

[30] In particular, the Habomai islets were occupied in the period of September 2 – 5, 1945. Kimura finds this significant because it occurred after the signing of the Japanese surrender on the USS Missouri in Tokyo Bay on September 2. See Kimura, *The Kurillian Knot*, 50.

[31] It is important to note that the directive included a disclaimer, specifically, "Nothing in this directive shall be construed as an indication of Allied policy relating to the ultimate determination of the minor islands referred to in Article 8 of the Potsdam Declaration." See the Joint Compendium, http://www.mofa.go.jp/region/europe/russia/territory/edition92/index.html (accessed January 13, 2012).

[32] See endnote 1, which describes the geologic terms of Lesser Kurile Ridge and Greater Kurile Ridge. In MacArthur's Directive Number 677, he defines "Kurile Islands" as the Greater Kurile Ridge.

[33] *Joint Compendium*, http://www.mofa.go.jp/region/europe/russia/territory/edition92/index.html (accessed January 13, 2012).

[34] Kimura, *The Kurillian Knot*, 52.

[35] Stephan, *The Kuril Islands*, 170.

[36] Kimura, *The Kurillian Knot*, 60.

[37] Some of the reasons the Soviet Union did not agree with the March draft were that it did not recognize the People's Republic of China, did not prevent future Japanese militarization, and that it provided for U.S. military forces to remain in Japan. As a result, the United States and Great Britain revised the draft in July, which became the San Francisco Peace Treaty. It specifically required that, "Japan renounces all right, title and claim to the Kurile Islands, and to that portion of Sakhalin and the islands adjacent to it over which Japan acquired sovereignty as a consequence of the Treaty of Portsmouth of September 5, 1905." However, the treaty did not stipulate to whom the territory would transfer to. The March draft had articulated to the Soviet Union. However, the revision was non-specific with respect to the Soviet Union, because the United States did not expect the Soviet delegation to sign it, due to their previous protest. In fact, the treaty included a provision that specifically ensured that any non-signatories to treaty were not entitled to any benefits from it. The specific wording is, "For the purposes of the present Treaty the Allied Powers shall be the States at war with Japan, or any State which previously formed a part of the territory of a State named in Article 23, provided that in each case the State concerned has signed and ratified the Treaty. Subject to the provisions of Article 21, the present Treaty shall not confer any rights, titles or benefits on any State which is not an Allied Power as herein defined; nor shall any right, title or interest of Japan be deemed to be diminished or prejudiced by any provision of the Treaty in favor of a State which is not an Allied Power as so defined." See Kimura, *The Kurillian Knot*, 58-61. These positions are also detailed in Andrey Gromyko's statement at the San Francisco Peace Conference. See Joint Compendium, http://www.mofa.go.jp/region/europe/russia/territory/edition92/index.html (accessed January 13, 2012).

[38] There were a total of 48 signatories to the Treaty.

[39] Kimura, *The Kurillian Knot*, 58-63.

[40] He stated, "Japan formally ratifies the territorial provisions of the Potsdam Surrender Terms... The Potsdam Surrender Terms constitute the only definition of peace terms to which, and by which, Japan and the Allied Powers as a whole are bound. There have been some private understandings between some Allied Governments; but by these Japan was not bound, nor were other Allies bound. Therefore, the treaty embodies article 8 of the Surrender Terms which provided that Japanese sovereignty should be limited to Honshu, Hokkaido, Kyushu, Shikoku and some minor islands... Some question has been raised as to whether the geographical name "Kurile Islands" mentioned in article 2 (c) includes the Habomai Islands. It is the view of the United States that it does not." The Potsdam Declaration upheld the Cairo Declaration, which began by renouncing territorial expansion as a goal of the Allies. However, it should be noted that the Soviet Union did not sign either the Cairo Declaration or the San Francisco Peace Treaty. Therefore, extending the concept of non-expansion to the Soviet Union is probably not supportable. Additionally, some definitions of the Habomai Islands includes Shikotan. See *Joint Compendium*, http://www.mofa.go.jp/region/europe/russia/territory/edition92/index.html (accessed January 13, 2012). Also see See Kimura, *The Kurillian Knot*, 59.

[41] Gromyko stated, "The peace treaty with Japan should, naturally, resolve a number of territorial questions connected with the peace settlement with Japan." This statement supports the concept of international law that only treaties determine sovereignty. He also stated, "Similarly, by attempting to violate grossly the sovereign rights of the Soviet Union regarding Southern Sakhalin and the islands adjacent to it, as well as the Kurile Islands already under the sovereignty of the Soviet Union, the draft also confines itself to a mere mention of the renunciation by Japan of rights, title and claims to these territories and makes no mention of the historic appurtenance of these territories and the indisputable obligation on the part of Japan to recognize the sovereignty of the Soviet Union over these parts of the territory of the USSR." Kimura provides a further significant fact supporting this concept of transfer of title by a two part process of renouncing and granting sovereignty over a territory. The San Francisco Peace Treaty resulted in a similar lack of conclusiveness to Taiwan and the Paracel Islands as it did with the Kurile Islands. Taiwan was only resolved by the Treaty of Peace between Japan and the Republic of China of 1952. Likewise, the Paracel Islands remain unresolved because there has never been a proper treaty to determine their title. See *Joint Compendium*, http://www.mofa.go.jp/region/europe/russia/territory/edition92/index.html (accessed January 13, 2012). Also see Kimura, *The Kurillian Knot*, 59-63.

[42] Prime Minister Yoshida stated, "With respect to the Kuriles and South Sakhalin, I cannot yield to the claim of the Soviet Delegate that Japan had grabbed them by aggression. At the time of the opening of Japan, her ownership of two islands of Etorofu and Kunashiri of the South Kuriles was not questioned at all by the Czarist government. But the North Kuriles north of Urruppu and the southern half of Sakhalin were areas open to both Japanese and Russian settlers. On May 7, 1875 the Japanese and Russian Governments effected through peaceful negotiations an arrangement under which South Sakhalin was made Russian territory, and the North Kuriles were in exchange made Japanese territory." He also stated, "Even the islands of Habomai and Shikotan, constituting part of Hokkaido, one of Japan's four main islands..." See *Joint Compendium*, http://www.mofa.go.jp/region/europe/russia/territory/edition92/index.html (accessed January 13, 2012).

[43] In his memoirs, Khrushchev stated it was a mistake not to sign the treaty, "Our interests were totally taken care of there. All we had to do was sign,...we would have gotten everything

we were promised…We should have signed. I don't know why we didn't…Since we had absolutely no contacts with Japan, our economy…suffered." Kimura, *The Kurillian Knot*, 64.

[44] Kimura, *The Kurillian Knot*, 66.

[45] Ibid.

[46] Ibid.

[47] This position differs from his statement in 1951 at the San Francisco Peace Conference. Kimura provides an argument that if the terms of a treaty are confusing, the signatories to the treaty should provide further clarification. This argument gives Dulles' statement credibility. However, it is probably not legally sufficient. In addition, this statement only expresses the understanding of one of 48 signatories to the San Francisco Peace Treaty. Kimura does note that there has been no opposition to this opinion. See Kimura, *The Kurillian Knot*, 67-68.

[48] There is an interesting twist to this story. Between the second and third Soviet – Japanese meetings, the Japanese Foreign Minister engaged U.S. Secretary of State Dulles on the matter. Dulles' response was one of concern. He did not want Japan to negotiate a settlement with the Soviet Union for anything less than all four islands. Dulles went further to remind the Japanese Prime Minister of Article 26 of the San Francisco Peace Treaty which states, "Should Japan make a peace settlement on war claims settlement with any State granting that State greater advantages than those provided by the present treaty, those same advantages shall be extended to the parties to the present treaty." Dulles even threatened to demand U.S. sovereignty to the Ryukyus (Okinawa) if Japan negotiated a two island settlement. Kimura asserts that this was most likely because of U.S. interests to have a problematic relationship between the Soviet Union and Japan during the Cold War. See Kimura, *The Kurillian Knot*, 71-72. Most importantly, Russian leaders, in particular Putin, have most likely concluded that Japan would have agreed to a two island settlement, if Dulles had not intervened with such a strong directive to Japan. This is probably a significant contributing factor to Putin's continued insistence of a two island solution.

[49] At the last minute, in classic Soviet negotiating style, Khrushchev insisted on the removal of the words "including the territorial question." See Kimura, *The Kurillian Knot*, 73.

[50] *Joint Compendium*, http://www.mofa.go.jp/region/europe/russia/territory/edition92/index.html (accessed January 13, 2012).

[51] There were two letters that preceded the 1956 Joint Declaration, one from Japan to the Soviet Union and one in response. The Japanese letter stated, "…the Japanese Government assumes that negotiations on the conclusion of a peace treaty including the territorial issue will continue after the reestablishment of normal diplomatic relations between the two countries." The Soviet responded with, "the Soviet Government accepts the view of the Japanese Government referred to above and announces its agreement to continue negotiations on the conclusion of a peace treaty, which would also include the territorial issue, after the reestablishment of normal diplomatic relations." These letters are included in the Joint Compendium but were consistently downplayed by the Soviets. See Kimura, *The Kurillian Knot*, 72. Also see *Joint Compendium*,

http://www.mofa.go.jp/region/europe/russia/territory/edition92/index.html (accessed January 13, 2012).

[52] For example, in 1977 Brezhnev wrote, "Statements to the effect that there are 'unresolved problems in relations between our two countries with regard to territorial issues' are one-sided and inaccurate." See Kimura *The Kurillian Knot*, 84, 91, and 110.

[53] In 1964, while visiting Japan, the First Deputy Chairman of the Council of Ministers of the Soviet Union Anastas Mikoyan (just prior to becoming the Chairman of the Presidium of the Supreme Soviet of the Soviet Union) explained the Soviet interests with respect to Etorofu and Kunashiri by stating, "Etorofu and Kunashiri may only be small islands, but they are the gateway to Kamchatka and cannot be abandoned" and "For the Soviet Union they are necessary as a link with Kamchatka and so long as Japan and the United States have a military alliance we cannot ever consider returning them." See Kimura, *The Kurillian Knot*, 76-77.

[54] *Joint Compendium*, http://www.mofa.go.jp/region/europe/russia/territory/edition92/index.html (accessed January 13, 2012).

[55] Ibid.

[56] Ibid.

[57] As General Secretary of the Communist Party of the Soviet Union, March 11, 1985 – August 24, 1991, and as Head of State of the Soviet Union, October 1, 1988 – December 25, 1991, Mikhail Gorbachev embarked on policies of perestroika (restructuring) and glasnost (openness). During his tenure, the Soviet Union withdrew from Afghanistan (1988-1989), the Intermediate Range Nuclear Forces (INF) Treaty was concluded (1988), additional reductions of nuclear forces under Strategic Arms Reduction Treaty (START) were negotiated, and allowed the Eastern Bloc nations to determine their own internal affairs (1988), which ended the Cold War and led to fall of the Berlin Wall. His final achievement was the dissolution of the Soviet Union and the creation of the Commonwealth of Independent States (CIS).

[58] Kimura, *The Kurillian Knot*, 92-94.

[59] Ibid, 94.

[60] Ibid, 93.

[61] Ibid, 102.

[62] There were an equal number of setbacks though. In 1987, there were two national security scandals: the alleged sale of submarine propeller technology to the USSR and the arrest of two Japanese Self Defense Force officers for the sale of intelligence related to the basing of U.S. fighter aircraft in Japan. See Kimura, *The Kurillian Knot*, 94-95.

[63] Foreign Minister Gromyko visited Japan in 1976 and Foreign Minister Sonada visited Moscow in 1978. Foreign Minister Shevardnadze visited Japan in January, 1986, followed by Foreign Minister Abe visiting Moscow in May, 1986. A second exchange occurred with Shevardnadze's visit in December, 1988 followed by Foreign Minister Uno's visit to Moscow in

May, 1989. Foreign Minister Shevardnadze's third visit to Japan was in September, 1990, followed by Foreign Minister Nakayama's visit to Moscow in January, 1991. See Kimura, *The Kurillian Knot*, 94-95.

[64] Ministry of Foreign Affairs of Japan, *Diplomatic Bluebook*, linked from the Ministry of Foreign Affairs of Japan Home Page http://www.mofa.go.jp/policy/other/bluebook/1987/1987-3-6.htm (accessed January 13, 2012).

[65] *Diplomatic Bluebook*, http://www.mofa.go.jp/policy/other/bluebook/1989/1989-3-6.htm (accessed January 13, 2012).

[66] Economic trade included steel from Japan and timber and coal from the Soviet Union. See Kimura, *The Kurillian Knot*, 96-97 and *Ministry of Foreign Affairs of Japan, Diplomatic Bluebook*, http://www.mofa.go.jp/policy/other/bluebook/1987/1987-3-6.htm (accessed January 13, 2012).

[67] Kimura, *The Kurillian Knot*, 105.

[68] *Joint Compendium*, http://www.mofa.go.jp/region/europe/russia/territory/edition92/index.html (accessed January 13, 2012).

[69] Kimura provides an assessment that the development of longer range submarine launched ballistic missiles in the 1980s enabled the Soviet Union to reach all of the United States from the Barents Sea, reducing the strategic imperative of a safe haven in the Sea of Okhotsk. See Kimura, 100-101. Author research determined that the Soviets deployed the R-29RL missile in 1979, with a range of 6,500 km and launched from a Delta III submarine. In 1983 and 1986, the Soviets fielded the R-39 and the R-29RM missiles with ranges of 8,300 km and launched from Typhoon and Delta IV submarines respectively. Six Typhoon submarines entered service from 1981 to 1989; at least the first two served in the northern fleet. Seven Delta IV submarines entered service between 1984 and 1990; all served in the northern fleet. This makes Kimura's assessment plausible. See Anatoly Zak, *RussianSpaceWeb.com: News and History of Astronautics in the Former USSR Home Page*, http://www.russianspaceweb.com/rockets_slbm.html (accessed January 13, 2012).

[70] *Joint Compendium*, http://www.mofa.go.jp/region/europe/russia/territory/edition92/index.html (accessed January 13, 2012).

[71] Kimura asserts that Gorbachev missed six opportunities to visit Japan under more favorable conditions for a wider reaching agreement. He further asserts that Gorbachev's focus had shifted from the "initiative" to "representative," perhaps because Gorbachev's rival, Boris Yeltsin, was elected chairman of the Russian Federated Soviet Socialist Republic on May 29, 1990, and Gorbachev was faced with a situation of a dual power structure by the time of the summit. Kimura provides an interesting counter-factual discussion of what could have happened if Gorbachev had taken more initiative to resolve the dispute and conclude a peace treaty. See Kimura, *The Kurillian Knot*, 101-102.

[72] At that time, Mikhail Gorbachev was the Chairman of the Supreme Soviet (head of state).

[73] Kimura, *The Kurillian Knot*, 103.

[74] Ibid, 103-104.

[75] *Diplomatic Bluebook*, http://www.mofa.go.jp/policy/other/bluebook/1992/1992-3-4.htm (accessed January 13, 2012).

[76] Kimura, *The Kurillian Knot*, 104.

[77] Ibid, 105.

[78] *Joint Compendium*, http://www.mofa.go.jp/region/europe/russia/territory/edition92/index.html (accessed January 13, 2012).

[79] Ibid.

[80] Kimura, *The Kurillian Knot*, 105-106.

[81] *Diplomatic Bluebook*, http://www.mofa.go.jp/policy/other/bluebook/1992/1992-3-4.htm (accessed January 13, 2012).

[82] *Hokkaido Committee to Promote Exchanges with the Four Northern Islands Home Page*, http://www.pref.hokkaido.lg.jp/sm/hrt/hp-en/toriku-en.htm (accessed January 13, 2012).

[83] *Diplomatic Bluebook*, http://www.mofa.go.jp/policy/other/bluebook/1992/1992-3-4.htm (accessed January 13, 2012).

[84] Ibid.

[85] Ibid.

[86] Kimura, *The Kurillian Knot*, 107.

[87] Jeffrey Mankoff, *Russian Foreign Policy: The Return of Great Power Politics*, A Council on Foreign Relations Book (New York, NY: Rowman & Littlefield Publishers, Inc., 2009), 29.

[88] Kimura, *The Kurillian Knot*, 108.

[89] Ibid, 5. Also see *Diplomatic Bluebook*, http://www.mofa.go.jp/policy/other/bluebook/1992/1992-3-4.htm (accessed January 13, 2012).

[90] Ministry of Foreign Affairs of Japan and Ministry of Foreign Affairs of the Russian Federation, *Joint Compendium of Documents on the History of Territorial Issue between Japan and Russia,* First Edition (1992), http://www.mofa.go.jp/region/europe/russia/territory/edition92/index.html (accessed January 13, 2012). It consists of a preface and the following 35 documents, ordered chronologically:
Preface
Map of Japan from the Shoho period (1644)
"Sketches of the Sea Islands", I. Kozyrevsky (1713)
Instruction from the collegium of the Admiralty to G.I. Mulovsky (1787)

Effective Japanese administration of the four Northern Islands in the late 18th-early 19th centuries

Decree by Emperor Alexander I (1821)

Instruction from Emperor Nicholas I to Putiatin (1853)

Article 2 of the Treaty of Commerce, Navigation and Delimitation between Japan and Russia (1855)

Article 2 of the Treaty for the Exchange of Sakhalin for the Kurile Islands (1875)

Article 18 of the Treaty on Commerce and Navigation between Japan and Russia, and Declaration (1895)

Article 9 of the Portsmouth Peace Treaty (1905)

Article 2 of the Convention on Fundamental Principles for Relations between Japan and the USSR, and Declaration (1925)

Neutrality Pact between Japan and the USSR (1941)

Atlantic Charter (1941)

Declaration of the Soviet Government regarding a participation to the Atlantic Charter (1941)

Cairo Declaration (1943)

Roosevelt-Stalin meeting during the Yalta Conference (1945)

Yalta Agreement (1945)

Announcement from the Soviet Government on the Denunciation of the Neutrality Pact (1945)

Potsdam Declaration (1945)

Announcement from the Soviet Government to the Government of Japan on the declaration of war (1945)

Announcement from the Japanese Government (1945)

Memorandum from the Commander-in-Chief of the Allied Forces to the Japanese Imperial Government (1946)

Decree of the Presidium of the USSR Supreme Soviet on the Creation of the South-Sakhalin Province in the Khabarovsk Region (1946)

Statement of the Delegate of the USA, John Dulles, at the Conference in San Francisco (1951)

Statement of the First Deputy Minister of Foreign Affairs of the USSR A.A. Gromyko, at the Conference in San Francisco (1951)

Statement of the Prime Minister of Japan, S. Yoshida, at the Conference in San Francisco (1951)

Articles 2 and 25 of the San Francisco Peace Treaty (1951)

Letter from the Plenipotentiary Representative of the Japanese Government, S. Matsumoto, to the USSR First Deputy Minister of Foreign Affairs, A.A. Gromyko (1956)

Letter from the USSR First Deputy Minister of Foreign Affairs, A.A. Gromyko, to the Plenipotentiary Representative of the Government of Japan, S. Matsumoto (1956)

Paragraph 9 of the Joint Declaration of Japan and the USSR (1956)

Memorandum from the Soviet Government to the Government of Japan (1960)

Memorandum from the Japanese Government to the Soviet Government (1960)

Japanese-Soviet Joint Communiqué (1973)

Japanese-Soviet Joint Communiqué (1991)

Letter from the President of the Russian Federation, B.N. Yeltsin, to the Russian People (1991)

[91] *Joint Compendium*, http://www.mofa.go.jp/region/europe/russia/territory/edition01/agreement.html (accessed January 13, 2012).

[92] Kimura, *The Kurillian Knot*, xi.

[93] Ibid, 111.

[94] *Diplomatic Bluebook*, http://www.mofa.go.jp/policy/other/bluebook/1992/1992-3-4.htm (accessed January 13, 2012).

[95] Inside the 12 nautical mile territorial sea limit established by the United Nations Convention on the Law of the Sea (UNCLOS). Although not at the time, both Japan and Russia are now signatories and have ratified the treaty (Japan: June 20, 1996 and Russia: March 12, 1997).

[96] "Russo-Japanese Conflict in the Kuril Islands", *Washington Post*, August 16, 1994, in ProQuest (accessed November 12, 2011).

[97] *Diplomatic Bluebook*, http://www.mofa.go.jp/policy/other/bluebook/1995/chp3.html#3 (accessed January 13, 2012).

[98] *Diplomatic Bluebook*, http://www.mofa.go.jp/policy/other/bluebook/1997/I-b.html#4 (accessed January 13, 2012).

[99] Kimura, *The Kurillian Knot*, 112.

[100] Kimura, *The Kurillian Knot*, 113. Also see *Diplomatic Bluebook*, http://www.mofa.go.jp/policy/other/bluebook/1998/I-b.html#3 (accessed January 13, 2012).

[101] Kimura, *The Kurillian Knot*, 114. Also see *Diplomatic Bluebook*, http://www.mofa.go.jp/policy/other/bluebook/1998/I-b.html#3 (accessed January 13, 2012).

[102] Russia joined APEC one year later, November 1998.

[103] *Diplomatic Bluebook*, http://www.mofa.go.jp/policy/other/bluebook/1998/I-b.html#3 (accessed January 13, 2012).

[104] *Diplomatic Bluebook*, http://www.mofa.go.jp/policy/other/bluebook/1999/I-c.html#2 (accessed January 13, 2012).

[105] *Joint Compendium*, http://www.mofa.go.jp/region/europe/russia/territory/edition01/agreement.html (accessed January 13, 2012).

[106] Kimura, *The Kurillian Knot*, 114.

[107] *Diplomatic Bluebook*, http://www.mofa.go.jp/policy/other/bluebook/1999/I-c.html#2 (accessed January 13, 2012).

[108] Kimura, *The Kurillian Knot*, 116.

[109] *Joint Compendium,*
http://www.mofa.go.jp/region/europe/russia/territory/edition01/moscow.html (accessed January 13, 2012).

[110] Politics, economy, security, culture and tourism, international cooperation, and environment.

[111] *Joint Compendium,*
http://www.mofa.go.jp/region/europe/russia/territory/edition01/moscow.html (accessed January 13, 2012).

[112] Ministry of Foreign Affairs of Japan and Ministry of Foreign Affairs of the Russian Federation, *New Edition of the Joint Compendium of Documents on the History of Territorial Issue between Japan and Russia,* New Edition (2001), http://www.mofa.go.jp/region/europe/russia/territory/edition01/index.html (accessed January 13, 2012). It consists of a preface and the following seven documents, ordered chronologically:
Preface
Tokyo Declaration on Japan-Russia Relations (October 1993)
Agreement between the Government of Japan and the Government of the Russian Federation on some matters of cooperation in the field of fishing operations for marine living resources (February 1998)
Note Verbale presented by the Embassy of Japan in the Russian Federation regarding visits without visas to the islands of Etorofu, Kunashiri, Shikotan and Habomai, aimed at providing emergency humanitarian assistance (September 1998)
Moscow Declaration on Establishing a Creative Partnership between Japan and the Russian Federation (November 1998)
Note Verbale presented by the Ministry of Foreign Affairs of Japan regarding the framework, streamlined to the maximum extent possible, for visits to the islands of Etorofu, Kunashiri, Shikotan and Habomai by Japanese nationals who are former residents and members of their families (September 1999)
Japan-Russia Cooperation Program on the Development of Joint Economic Activities in the islands of Etorofu, Kunashiri, Shikotan and Habomai (September 2000)
Statement by the Prime Minister of Japan and the President of the Russian Federation on the Issue of a Peace Treaty (September 2000)

[113] *Ministry of Foreign Affairs of Japan Home Page,*
http://www.mofa.go.jp/region/europe/russia/pmv0301/plan.html (accessed January 13, 2012).

[114] *Prime Minister of Japan and His Cabinet Home Page,*
http://www.kantei.go.jp/foreign/koizumiphoto/2004/09/02hoppou_e.html (accessed January 13, 2012).

[115] *Ministry of Foreign Affairs of Japan Home Page,*
http://www.mofa.go.jp/policy/economy/summit/2005/russia.html (accessed January 13, 2012).

[116] *Ministry of Foreign Affairs of Japan Home Page,*
http://www.mofa.go.jp/announce/announce/2006/2/0223.html (accessed January 13, 2012).

[117] *Ministry of Foreign Affairs of Japan Home Page,*
http://www.mofa.go.jp/announce/announce/2007/2/0209-2.html (accessed January 13, 2012).

[118] *Ministry of Foreign Affairs of Japan Home Page*, http://www.mofa.go.jp/announce/announce/2006/8/0817.html, (accessed January 13, 2012). Also see *Ministry of Foreign Affairs of Japan Home Page*, http://www.mofa.go.jp/announce/announce/2006/8/0829-3.html, (accessed January 13, 2012) and *Ministry of Foreign Affairs of Japan Home Page*, http://www.mofa.go.jp/announce/announce/2006/8/0830.html (accessed January 13, 2012).

[119] Fred Weir, "More Turf Wars for Japan After Russia's Medvedev Visits Disputed Kuril Islands," Christian Science Monitor, November 1, 2010, in ProQuest (accessed November 12, 2011).

[120] Author Not Provided, "Medvedev Dismisses Japanese Concerns over Kuril Visits," RIA Novosti, February 4, 2011, http://en.rian.ru/russia/20110204/162456230.html (accessed February 17, 2012).

[121] Author Not Provided, "Broadsides from Broadsheets: Japan and the Kuril Islands," Economist, February 7, 2011, in ProQuest (accessed November 12, 2011).

[122] Fred Weir, "Russia's Renewed Focus on Kuril Islands Draws Japanese Ire," Christian Science Monitor, February 11, 2011, in ProQuest (accessed November 12, 2011).

[123] The conflicts include the Japanese intervention in the Russian Far East during the revolution following World War I (1917-1921), the Japanese occupation of northern Sakhalin (1920-1925), or the fighting between Soviet and Japanese forces on the Soviet-Manchurian border (1938) or in Outer Mongolia (1939). See Geoffrey Jukes, "Can the Southern Kuriles Be Demilitarized?" in *Northern Territories, Asia-Pacific Regional Conflicts and the Åland Experience: Untying the Kurillian Knot*, ed. Kimie Hara and Geoffrey Jukes (New York, NY: Routledge, 2009), 65.

[124] Kimura, *The Kurillian Knot*, 44 and 51-52.

[125] Jukes, "Can the Southern Kuriles Be Demilitarized?" 65.

[126] Ibid, 66.

[127] Hipokappu Bay is the smaller of the two bases. It is Russia's southern Kurile sonar tracking station and reports to Petropavlovsk. It also includes an airfield (Burevestnik) and is intended as a dispersal staging area for ships from Sakhalin (Korsakov) and Petropavlovsk. The other base is Burotan Bay, on the island of Simushir. This port includes the stationing of naval vessels and is ice free year round. See Jukes, "Can the Southern Kuriles Be Demilitarized?" 68, 72, and 74.

[128] Petropavlovsk is on the eastern side of the Kamchatka peninsula, and therefore has direct access to the Pacific Ocean. This can be interpreted as a vulnerability to U.S. attack submarines.

[129] Jukes, "Can the Southern Kuriles Be Demilitarized?" 67-68.

[130] The author notes that the New START treaty was signed in 2010. It limits the number of launch tubes, but does not limit the number of submarines. Therefore, it does not add or detract from Jukes' argument. It does serve to extend the expiration of SORT in 2012 by 10 years.

[131] Russia is building new SSBNs, however these are replacements of aging submarines, not an expansion. Russia's SSBN fleet size of 12 provides sufficient capability and is not likely to increase. In 1996 Russia began construction of a new class of SSBNs, the Borei class. The first submarine is complete, but has not been outfitted with missiles yet. A second submarine began construction in 2004 and a third in 2006. These submarines are likely replacements for the aging Delta III SSBNs, which entered service between 1976 and 1982 and are now being retired. Of the 14 Delta IIIs built, four are still in service, in the Pacific Fleet. The four Delta IIIs comprise all of the Pacific Fleet's SSBN capability. The balance of Russia's 12 SSBNs are in the Northern Fleet. Of the eight SSBNs, five are operational and three are in overhaul, refit, or conducting testing. There are no SSBNs in the Baltic or Black Sea fleets. See *Russian Strategic Nuclear Forces Home Page*, http://russianforces.org/navy/ (accessed March 3, 2012).

[132] Jukes, "Can the Southern Kuriles Be Demilitarized?" 62-64 and 67-68.

[133] Ibid, 69.

[134] Jukes, "Can the Southern Kuriles Be Demilitarized?" 72.

[135] Ibid, 73.

[136] Jukes provided the information that the Vries Strait (sometimes described as the Friz or Etorofu Strait) was the southern most of four straits used by U.S. submarines in 1982 and further stated that the straits between Etorofu and Kunashiri (Yekaterin Strait) and Kunashiri and Hokkaido (Nemuro Strait) are not suitable for submarines due to depth and physical curvature. A second source provides a slightly different assessment of the strategic importance of the straits. Allison et al. describe the Vries Strait, which was the boundary agreed upon in the 1855 Treaty of Shimoda, as 35 kilometers wide and 625 meters (2,050 feet) deep. This source goes on to further describe that in peace time Russian surface and submarine forces use five straits to transit between the Sea of Okhotsk and the Pacific Ocean, including three in the undisputed Kurile Islands, the Vries Strait, and the Yekaterin Strait between Etorofu and Kunashiri. See Graham Allison, Hiroshi Kimura, and Konstantin Sarkisov, eds., *Beyond Cold War to Trilateral Cooperation in the Asia-Pacific Region: Scenarios for New Relationships Between Japan, Russia, and the United States*, (Cambridge, MA: Strengthening Democratic Institutions Project, Harvard University, 1972), 9-10.

[137] Jukes, "Can the Southern Kuriles Be Demilitarized?" 73. Also see Allison, et al., *Beyond Cold War to Trilateral Cooperation in the Asia-Pacific Region*, 10.

[138] Allison, et al., *Beyond Cold War to Trilateral Cooperation in the Asia-Pacific Region*, ix, 10.

[139] Jukes, "Can the Southern Kuriles Be Demilitarized?" 74.

[140] Ibid, 70-71.

[141] Allison, et al., *Beyond Cold War to Trilateral Cooperation in the Asia-Pacific Region*, ix, 10.

[142] The initiative included air defense missiles, tanks, and communications equipment in 2011. Military infrastructure construction is ongoing on the islands of Etorofu and Kunashiri. Anti-ship missiles will be deployed to the islands no later than 2015. The initiative is focused on military hardware; it does not include an increase in personnel. See Author Not Provided, "Russia to Step Up Military Presence on Kuril Islands - Medvedev," RIA Novosti Online, February 9, 2011, http://en.rian.ru/russia/20110209/162521531.html (accessed February 17, 2012). Also see Author Not Provided, "State-of-the-art re-armament for Kuril Islands," RT Online October 12, 2011, http://rt.com/politics/kuril-islands-defense-tanks-663/ (accessed March 12, 2012).

[143] An assessment in 2007 was that the islands had lost their former military significance. See Markku Heiskanen, "Solving the Territorial Dispute Between Japan and Russia: The Åland Islands and Finland's Post-World War II Experiences as a Source of Inspiration" in *Northern Territories, Asia-Pacific Regional Conflicts and the Åland Experience: Untying the Kurillian Knot*, ed. Kimie Hara and Geoffrey Jukes (New York, NY: Routledge, 2009), 108 and 110. The author does not see any reason that re-establishes their military significance since 2007.

[144] Kimura, *The Kurillian Knot*, 46.

[145] Konstantin Sarkisov, "The Territorial Dispute Between Japan and Russia: The 'Two Island Solution' and Putin's Last Years as President", in *Northern Territories, Asia-Pacific Regional Conflicts and the Åland Experience: Untying the Kurillian Knot*, ed. Kimie Hara and Geoffrey Jukes (New York, NY: Routledge, 2009), 49.

[146] Brad Williams, *Resolving the Russo-Japanese Territorial Dispute: Hokkaido-Sakhalin Relations*, Routledge Japanese Studies Series (New York, NY: Routledge, 2007), 153.

[147] Author Not Provided, "Putin's Russia, Call Back Yesterday," The Economist, March 3, 2012, 31-34.

[148] This paragraph summarizes analysis presented by Williams, *Resolving the Russo-Japanese Territorial Dispute*, 145-153.

[149] The Japanese partners first appealed to the Sakhalin Arbitration Court, which upheld the St. Petersburg Arbitration Court's ruling. See Williams, *Resolving the Russo-Japanese Territorial Dispute*, 151.

[150] Williams, *Resolving the Russo-Japanese Territorial Dispute*, 152.

[151] Dmitri Trenin, *Post-Imperium: A Eurasian Story* (Washington DC: Carnegie Endowment for International Peace, 2011), 137.

[152] As of this writing, only 2 of Japan's 54 nuclear power plants are in operation.

[153] Nancy Birdsall and Francis Fukuyama, "The Post-Washington Consensus: Development After the Crisis," *Foreign Affairs* 90, no. 2 (March/April 2011), in ProQuest (accessed March 9, 2012).

[154] Ibid.

[155] These currents are analogous to the Gulf Stream and the Labrador currents meeting in the North Atlantic Ocean and creating the rich fishing grounds of the Grand Banks and Flemish Cap.

[156] There are potential mineral deposits in the EEZ offshore and on the disputed islands; however, these resources are not being extracted at this time. Expectations of future exploitation are minimal, due to quantities, mining costs, and the extreme climate. The resources do not include oil or natural gas.

[157] Japan ratified the *Convention* and the *Agreement Relating to the Implementation of Part XI* in 1996. Japan ratified the *1995 United Nations Fish Stocks Agreement* in 2006. Russia ratified all three instruments in 1997. The *Convention* was negotiated in 1982 and went into force in 1994. See the "Oceans and Law of the Sea" page, linked from the *United Nations Home Page*, http://www.un.org/depts/los/index.htm (accessed January 13, 2012).

[158] See Alex G. Oude Elferink, *The Law of Maritime Boundary Delimitation: A Case Study of the Russian Federation*, Publications on Ocean Development (Dordrecht, Netherlands: Martinus Nijhoff Publishers, 1994), 311. Also see the Sea Around Us Project, a scientific collaboration of the University of British Columbia and the Pew Environment Group, linked from http://www.seaaroundus.org/ (accessed January 13, 2012).

[159] Williams, *Resolving the Russo-Japanese Territorial Dispute*, 155.

[160] In Japan, cars drive on the left side of the road, hence steering wheels are on the right side of the vehicle. In Russia, the driving and vehicles are of the same configuration as the United States (drive on the right, steering wheel on the left).

[161] Gilbert Rozman, "Cross-Border Relations and Russo-Japanese Bi-lateral Ties in the 1990s," in *Japan and Russia: The Tortuous Path to Normalization, 1949-1999*, ed. Gilbert Rozman (New York, NY: St. Martin's Press, 2000), 208.

[162] Williams, *Resolving the Russo-Japanese Territorial Dispute*, 60.

[163] The agreements are: the *Agreement on Mutual Relations in the Field of Fisheries off the coast of Both Countries between the Government of Japan and the Government of the Union of Soviet Socialist Republics*, signed in Tokyo on December 7, 1984; the *Agreement between the Government of Japan and the Government of the Union of Soviet Socialist Republics Concerning Cooperation in the Field of Fisheries*, signed in Moscow on May 12, 1985; and the *Agreement between the Government of Japan and the Government of the Russian Federation on some matters of cooperation in the field of fishing operations for marine living resources*, signed in Moscow on February 21, 1998.

[164] Williams, *Resolving the Russo-Japanese Territorial Dispute*, 37-38.

[165] Williams, *Resolving the Russo-Japanese Territorial Dispute*, 154. Also, since Russia has begun to use force, and in particular after the August 2006 incident that resulted in the death of a Japanese crewmember, the Japanese government has directed Japanese fishing vessels to not fish in the disputed waters. See Hiroshi Kimura, "The Northern Territories Issue: Japanese-

Russian Relations and Domestic Concerns in Japan," in *Northern Territories, Asia-Pacific Regional Conflicts and the Åland Experience: Untying the Kurillian Knot*, ed. Kimie Hara and Geoffrey Jukes (New York, NY: Routledge, 2009), 32.

[166] Williams, *Resolving the Russo-Japanese Territorial Dispute*, 155.

[167] Ibid, 160-161.

[168] Rozman, "Cross-Border Relations and Russo-Japanese Bi-lateral Ties in the 1990s," 206.

[169] Williams, *Resolving the Russo-Japanese Territorial Dispute*, 156.

[170] Ibid, 164.

[171] Ibid, 161.

[172] Ibid, 157.

[173] Ibid, 159.

[174] Ibid, 157.

[175] Ibid, 45.

[176] Kimura, "The Northern Territories Issue," 32.

[177] Joint Compendium, http://www.mofa.go.jp/region/europe/russia/territory/edition01/agreement.html (accessed January 13, 2012).

[178] Williams, *Resolving the Russo-Japanese Territorial Dispute*, 30.

[179] Ibid, 21 and 159-160.

[180] Ibid, 110.

[181] Ibid, 21.

[182] Ibid, 157-158.

[183] Ibid, 160.

[184] Ibid, 161-163.

[185] Ibid, 166.

[186] Ibid, 154.

[187] Ibid, 158 and 165.

[188] Ibid, 159.

[189] Ibid, 158.

[190] *Ministry of Foreign Affairs of Japan Home Page,* http://www.mofa.go.jp/announce/announce/2001/8/0803-3.html (accessed January 13, 2012).

[191] As of 2009, South Korea and China both had positive, although declining, population growth rates. Both Russia and Japan have negative, and declining, population growth rates. See the World Bank's population growth data at http://data.worldbank.org/indicator/SP.POP.GROW

[192] Williams, *Resolving the Russo-Japanese Territorial Dispute,* 121.

[193] Allison, et al., *Beyond Cold War to Trilateral Cooperation in the Asia-Pacific Region,* ix, 10.

[194] Williams, *Resolving the Russo-Japanese Territorial Dispute,* 160-161.

[195] Kimura, "The Northern Territories Issue," 31-32.

[196] Both industries are important at the regional level.

[197] Especially since only 2 of 54 nuclear power plants are currently online and are scheduled to come offline in 2012, in the wake of the Fukushima Daiichi disaster.

[198] The importance to Japan of diversification of its suppliers is exemplified by the fact that the Japanese government set a maximum limit of 10% of oil and natural gas from Russia. See Trenin, *Post-Imperium,* 169.

[199] Transneft's objective is to transport 30 to 80 million tons of oil per year (600,000 to 1,600,000 barrels per day). See Trenin, *Post-Imperium,* 169.

[200] Trenin, *Post-Imperium,* 169.

[201] Kimura, "The Northern Territories Issue," 33-34.

[202] Development began in 1994 of the oil and natural gas fields offshore the northeast coast of Sakhalin, in the Sea of Okhotsk. Today, it consists of three platforms, onshore processing facilities, and pipelines that transport the oil and gas to the southern end of Sakhalin for export at the port of Prigorodnoye in Aniva Bay. The international consortium, Sakhalin Energy, was restructured in 2007, to provide Gazprom with a majority share (50% plus one share), with Royal Dutch Shell and two Japanese firms retaining the balance of the shares; Japanese interests are 22.5%.

[203] *Gazprom Home Page,* http://www.gazprom.com/about/production/projects/deposits/ (accessed January 13, 2012).

[204] *Sakhalin Energy Home Page,* http://www.sakhalinenergy.ru/en/ (accessed January 13, 2012).

[205] Akio Kawato, "Overcoming the Legacy of History: Japanese Public Relations in *Russia, 1990-1994*" in *Japan and Russia: The Tortuous Path to Normalization, 1949-1999*, ed. Gilbert Rozman (New York, NY: St. Martin's Press, 2000), 325.

[206] For examples of last minute changes, such as Khrushchev and the 1956 Joint Declaration, see Kimura, *The Kurillian Knot*, 73, and the 1973 Joint Communiqué, see Kimura, *The Kurillian Knot*, 84. For a discussion of "cherry picking", see Kimura, *The Kurillian Knot*, 76. For "bazaar" style bargaining and resultant 50-50 split, see Kimura, *The Kurillian Knot*, 134-135.

[207] Kawato, "Overcoming the Legacy of History," 325.

[208] Williams, *Resolving the Russo-Japanese Territorial Dispute*, 11-18.

[209] Richard D. Lewis, *When Cultures Collide: Leading Across Cultures*, 3rd ed. (Boston, MA: Nicholas Brealey International, 2006).

[210] Lewis makes the following observations of Russian culture which have relevance to resolving the territorial dispute: "disrespect for edicts, …blunt in speech, …centralized authority, …characteristics of caution, tenacity, and reticence, …negotiate like they play chess: they plan several moves ahead, …proud people and do not like to be humiliated, …do not expect them to be open to straightforward debate, …they rebel if they feel the pressure is intolerable." He also observes, "Their preferred tactic in case of deadlock is to display patience and 'sit it out'; they will only abandon this tactic if the other side shows great firmness," and "Personal relationships…can often achieve miracles in cases of apparent official deadlock." Finally, he states that Russians are "warm, emotional, caring people, eagerly responding to kindness and love, once they perceive that they are not being 'taken in' one more time." See Lewis, *When Cultures Collide*, 372-376.

[211] Lewis makes the following observations of Japanese culture which have relevance to resolving the territorial dispute: "ultra honesty, …punctuality,…Confucian hierarchy where ideas originate from below, …everything must be placed in context, …blunt language is too brief and out of place, …collective and representative, …do not like to lose face, …there is little flexibility in their position during a meeting, more evident between meetings, …meet force with intransigence." He also observes, "If great respect is shown and very reasonable demands are made, they are capable of modifying their own demands greatly." Finally, he states, "Logic and intellectual argument alone cannot sway the Japanese. They must like you and trust you wholeheartedly, otherwise no deal!" See Lewis, *When Cultures Collide*, 509-517.

[212] Kimura, *The Kurillian Knot*, 107.

[213] Ibid, 108.

[214] Ibid, 101-102 and 106.

[215] Williams, *Resolving the Russo-Japanese Territorial Dispute*, 141-143.

[216] Ibid, 142.

[217] Trenin, *Post-Imperium*, 137. Also see Author Not Provided, "Japan Accepts Russian Reason for Calling Halt to Aid for Kurils," RIA Novosti Online, August 7, 2009,

http://en.beta.rian.ru/world/20090807/155756722.html (accessed March 17, 2012) and Author Not Provided, "Japan to Stop Aid to Russia's South Kuril Islands," RIA Novosti Online, November 8, 2009, http://en.rian.ru/world/20091108/156752104.html (accessed March 17, 2012).

[218] Author Not Provided, "Medvedev Orders Deployment of Weapons on Kuril Islands," RT Online, February 9, 2011, http://rt.com/politics/kuril-islands-medvedev-weapon/ (accessed March 17, 2012).

[219] Kimura, "The Northern Territories Issue," 37.

[220] Ibid, 38.

[221] Kimura, "The Northern Territories Issue," 37. Also, it should be noted that since 1951, Japan has maintained this position. Additionally, although the status of the central and northern Kurile Islands remains undetermined, the San Francisco Peace Treaty does imply that the Soviet Union was the intended recipient of southern Sakhalin since the 1951 Treaty mentions the 1905 Treaty of Portsmouth, which was between Japan and Russia. See [221] Sarkisov, "The Territorial Dispute Between Japan and Russia," 49.

[222] Kimura, "The Northern Territories Issue," 37.

[223] Sarkisov, "The Territorial Dispute Between Japan and Russia," 44.

[224] Kimura, *The Kurillian Knot*, 158.

[225] Sarkisov, "The Territorial Dispute Between Japan and Russia," 41-42.

[226] Ibid, 42.

[227] It is assumed to have been proposed in 2001 between Putin and Prime Minister Yoshiro Mori. Ibid.

[228] Kosuke Takahashi, "Creative Thinking on the Kurils", *Asia Times Online*, April 20, 2005, http://www.atimes.com/atimes/Japan/GD20Dh03.html (accessed March 17, 2012).

[229] Kimura, *The Kurillian Knot*, 118-121.

[230] Sarkisov, "The Territorial Dispute Between Japan and Russia," 42.

[231] Ibid, 42.

[232] Ibid, 47.

[233] Kimie Hara, "Introduction", in *Northern Territories, Asia-Pacific Regional Conflicts and the Åland Experience: Untying the Kurillian Knot*, eds. Kimie Hara and Geoffrey Jukes (New York, NY: Routledge, 2009), 6.

[234] Ibid, 11.

[235] This is a neo-liberal perspective. See Hara, "Introduction," 6-7.

[236] The conference consisted of 19 academics, government bureaucrats, and military security officials from Australia, Canada, Denmark, Finland and Åland, Japan, Russia, Sweden, the United Kingdom, and the United States. The Åland Islands were contested between Sweden and Finland. Great Britain referred the dispute to the League of Nations, which provided a resolution in 1921. For a further description of the Aland dispute and resolution and the 2006 conference, see Kimie Hara and Geoffrey Jukes, eds., *Northern Territories, Asia-Pacific Regional Conflicts and the Åland Experience: Untying the Kurillian Knot* (New York, NY: Routledge, 2009), in particular the forward, Introduction, and Chapter 1.

[237] Hara, "Introduction," 7.

[238] Ibid, 10.

[239] The Six Party Talk nations are Russia, Japan, China, the United States, the Republic of Korea, and the Democratic People's Republic of Korea. Although specifically focused on the North Korean nuclear situation, there is a broader concern of North East Asian security. Furthermore, it is the only multi-lateral regional security organization; APEC and the ASEAN Regional Forum (ARF) are predominantly economic forums. See Hara, "Introduction," 7. Also see Hara, "Envisioning Åland Inspired Solutions for the Northern Territories Problem," in *Northern Territories, Asia-Pacific Regional Conflicts and the Åland Experience: Untying the Kurillian Knot*, ed. Kimie Hara and Geoffrey Jukes (New York, NY: Routledge, 2009), 118.

[240] Heiskanen, "Solving the Territorial Dispute Between Japan and Russia," 109.

[241] Hara, "Envisioning Åland Inspired Solutions for the Northern Territories Problem," 117.

[242] This approach could include Takeshima/Tokdo, the Senkaku/Diaoyu, Paracel, and Spratly islands. See Hara, "Envisioning Åland Inspired Solutions for the Northern Territories Problem," 117. Also see Hara, "Introduction," 1-4.

[243] Additional economic measures might include fishing rights, trade agreements, or economic assistance. Military concessions could include force limits or restrictions in the Kuriles or in Hokkaido.

[244] Heiskanen, "Solving the Territorial Dispute Between Japan and Russia," 110.

[245] Ibid, 110.

[246] Kimura, *The Kurillian Knot*, xxiii-xxiv. Also see Yakov Zinberg, "The Kuril Islands Dispute: Towards Dual Sovereignty," *IBRU Boundary and Security Bulletin* (Winter 1997-1998), 89-98.

[247] Hara, "Envisioning Åland Inspired Solutions for the Northern Territories Problem," 114.

[248] The Antarctic Treaty was originally signed on December 1,1959 by the 12 nations that had significant interest in Antarctica during the 1958-1959 season; Argentina, Australia, Belgium, Chile, France, Japan, New Zealand, Norway, South Africa, the Soviet Union, the Great Britain, and the United States. It became effective on June 23, 1961, and stipulates that Antarctica will be used for peaceful purposes only, such as scientific research, and prohibits military uses. It does not recognize, dispute, or establish any territorial sovereignty claims. It

also prevents new claims while the treaty is in force. At the time of signing, there were seven nations that had territorial claims and another two countries that withheld their right to make a claim in the future. See *Secretariat of the Antarctic Treaty Home Page*, http://www.ats.aq/e/ats.htm (accessed January 13, 2012).

[249] Multi-lateral agreements like the Antarctic Treaty are more durable than bi-lateral agreements. See Hara, "Envisioning Åland Inspired Solutions for the Northern Territories Problem," 118.

[250] Author Not Provided, "World Park Proposed for Kuril Islands", *National Parks* 66, no. 1-2 (January 1992), 15.

[251] Kimura, *The Kurillian Knot*, xxiv

[252] Hara, "Envisioning Åland Inspired Solutions for the Northern Territories Problem," 113-114.

[253] Sarkisov, "The Territorial Dispute Between Japan and Russia," 51.

[254] Lewis, *When Cultures Collide*, 372-376.

[255] Sarkisov, "The Territorial Dispute Between Japan and Russia," 45-46.

[256] Sometimes the term "50 - 50 split" is used to describe a literal equal split of land area. This concept would provide a physical land boundary on the island of Etorofu, about 3/4 Russian and 1/4 Japanese. This option does not seem as practical as a three island solution, since it adds the additional complication of a land boundary.

[257] Sarkisov, "The Territorial Dispute Between Japan and Russia," 45-46.

[258] This includes Kaliningrad (Germany), Pechenga and Karelia (Finland), areas in Amur and Trans-Baikal regions (China), the other Kurile islands and Sakhalin (Japan), and Leningrad and Russia's northwest provinces (Baltic states).

[259] Kimura, *The Kurillian Knot*, 148-149.

[260] Heiskanen, "Solving the Territorial Dispute Between Japan and Russia," 108-109.

[261] Jukes, "Can the Southern Kuriles Be Demilitarized?" 71.

[262] Kimura, *The Kurillian Knot*, 148.

[263] Sarkisov, "The Territorial Dispute Between Japan and Russia," 49.

[264] Kimura, *The Kurillian Knot*, xxvi-xxvii.

[265] Hara, "Envisioning Åland Inspired Solutions for the Northern Territories Problem," 114.

[266] Another example is the Sino-Soviet border conflict of 1969. In particular, the Zhenbao Island incident which appears relatively insignificant yet escalated to armed conflict and resulted in several hundred casualties.

[267] Hara, "Envisioning Åland Inspired Solutions for the Northern Territories Problem," 114.

[268] Ibid, 115.

[269] Ibid, 114.

[270] Kimura, "The Northern Territories Issue," 36.

[271] Weir, "More Turf Wars for Japan After Russia's Medvedev Visits Disputed Kuril Islands."

[272] Hara, "Envisioning Åland Inspired Solutions for the Northern Territories Problem," 115.

[273] Trenin, *Post-Imperium*, 43.

[274] After reviewing this dispute, there are several lessons that are worth reflecting upon. First is the specificity of language used in formal documents, agreements, and treaties. Diplomats and politicians are often purposely vague. It provides room for interpretation and enhances flexibility. Vague language can also promote confusion and allow for significant differences in opinion. Neither is right nor wrong. However, all relevant parties should understand the documents that they are bound to and the opportunities and challenges that may present themselves in the future. In this particular territorial dispute, it is certainly a valid assessment that vague language when referencing the "Kuril Islands" has contributed to the perpetuation of a dispute over four relatively insignificant islands, predominantly on the basis of principle and nationalism. The benefits of peace and normal relations between the then Soviet Union, now Russia and Japan that could have existed since 1951 surely outweigh the benefits of a dispute lasting more than 65 years. Another observation is that over the course of time, the strategic environment that influences a dispute changes. National interests and negotiating strengths change. This includes economic strength, geo-political considerations, domestic consensus, and military power. What is open to negotiation today may not be negotiable tomorrow.[274] There is some risk in leaving a dispute unresolved. Thus, disputing parties must carefully consider what they pass up. It is imaginable that many of the administrations in both countries would have settled earlier, if they understood the consequence was a deadlocked dispute that would be perpetuated ad infinitum. A third observation is that statements always matter. This includes interviews and information conveyed through the media. When used to one's advantage, these are informal mediums to present ideas and test ideas. When one is not cognizant of the impact of communication, one can transmit a message to an audience that it never meant to communicate. Fourth, it is always worthwhile to remember that international law upholds formal bi-lateral agreements as documented in joint declarations and treaties. Unilateral declarations are just statements and multi-lateral agreements have no bearing on anyone but the signatories. And finally, de facto arrangements can have a momentum of their own that make them almost as powerful as de jure arrangements.